As James I prepared to open Parliament in the first week of November, 1605, one of history's most famous conspiracies reached its climax – the Gunpowder Plot. For more than two years Robert Catesby had masterminded a plot to blow up the Houses of Parliament, as the signal for a great Catholic rebellion. The gunpowder was to be detonated by Guy Fawkes. But at the twelfth hour Fawkes was arrested and the plot collapsed.

Lewis Winstock has brought together a wealth of primary evidence, to piece together the events of this remarkable story. He shows how Catesby recruited his team, and traces the rows and disagreements, hopes and miscalculations, as the tiny band of conspirators struggled toward their goal. For at the eleventh hour a mysterious warning letter passed into the hands of the Privy Council, and armed guards hurriedly searched the cellars of Westminster, where the treason of "one base knave in a dark corner" was revealed. As the author shows, retribution was swift and savage. After a showpiece trial, the plotters were removed from the Tower and mercilessly hanged, drawn and quartered.

This new DOCUMENTARY HISTORY title gives a unique insight into the troubled character of Jacobean England, with its deep religious fears and social pressures.

Frontispiece Gunpowder Treason and Plot: the arrest of Guy Fawkes and the other conspirators (1605)

Gunpowder Treason and Plot

Lewis Winstock

WAYLAND PUBLISHERS · LONDON

G. P. PUTNAM'S SONS · NEW YORK

SBN (hardback): 85340 045 8

101 Grays Inn Road, London WC1
Set in 'Monophoto' Times and printed offset litho in Great Britain by
Page Bros (Norwich) Ltd, Norwich

Contents

The Illustrations

1 England Troubled

A definition of "The Plot"

"GUNPOWDER PLOT, the plot of a few Roman Catholics to blow up the Houses of Parliament on 5th November, 1605, while king, lords and commons were assembled there. The plot was devised by Robert Catesby, and Guy Fawkes was chosen to put it into execution. But it was betrayed and Fawkes arrested on 4th November. The conspirators who were taken alive were executed; Catesby was killed while resisting arrest." This is the account of the Gunpowder Plot in the Oxford Companion to English Literature, which is a highly respected and reliable reference book. It is a straight-forward statement of the kind that most students, and most of the general public, would accept. It is, in fact, substantially correct.

Two aspects of the Plot

But this simple paragraph gives no hint that the Plot is among the most baffling incidents in English history. It is possible to accept the outline of the Plot as it is given in the Oxford Companion, or it can be treated as something far more complicated. It is also the story of intelligence work and of conspirators who often did not tell each other the complete truth, and of agents working for one of history's greatest spy-masters – Robert Cecil, the Earl of Salisbury.

Even at the time of the Plot very few people understood what was happening. It was like a jig-saw puzzle, the pieces of which were either missing or would not fit. One of the best nineteenth-century historians of the Plot summed the situation up in these words: "The true history of the Gunpowder Plot is now known to no man . . . It is impossible to believe that the proceedings of the conspirators were actually such as they are related to have

Opposite The Catholic Queen of England, Mary I, with her husband, Philip II of Spain. After Mary's death in 1558, Philip became the most powerful Papal candidate for the English throne

been. It is unquestionable that the government consistently falsified the story and evidence presented to the world (1)."

Unreliable sources

Much of the difficulty in understanding the true nature of the Plot stems from the documents that concern it. After the Plot was revealed statements were taken by government officials from the surviving conspirators, from their servants and acquaintances, and from anyone else whom it was thought might have useful information. The officials were able to write down anything that sounded useful, and ignore anything that was awkward. We know that this is what they did. But sometimes when they took a second look at what had been written down, and a remark here or there seemed inconvenient, they ruthlessly scratched out or pasted over anything which did not fit in with their version of events.

Statements of Guy Fawkes and Winter

Despite the fact that King James I's government could select and change the available evidence, and could publish as many statements as it wanted, it preferred to print just two for the public's notice. One was the statement of Guy Fawkes whom we know was under great torture at the time. The other belongs to a conspirator named Thomas Winter. He, too, may have been tortured, but the striking thing is that the document which is believed to be his confession is almost certainly a forgery as his name is mis-spelt. Thomas wrote his surname "Wintour" whereas in the supposed confession it appears "Winter". The evidence in these two statements therefore has to be treated very cautiously, for it is not likely to be wholly true.

It may be wondered why, if the government was so ready to forge the evidence of one leading conspirator, it did not forge statements by the others. The explanation is that of the three chief conspirators, namely Robert Catesby, Thomas Percy and Thomas Winter, Catesby and Percy were killed when a sheriff's posse ran them to ground. Because the conspirators were outnumbered and did not use fire-arms it is probable that they could easily have been captured, and not killed. As it happened, they died from gunshot wounds inflicted from a distance, and their killer was handsomely rewarded. Perhaps he was paid for closing two mouths that might have embarrassed Robert Cecil. "Some people will not stick to report that the great statesman, sending to apprehend these traitors, gave special charge and directions for Percy and Catesby. 'Let me never see them alive' (2)."

Death of witnesses

Catesby and Percy were not the only men involved in the Gunpowder Plot who went to an untimely, or timely, end. Another conspirator of whom much more will be heard was Francis Tresham, and he died soon after his arrest, before a proper statement could be taken. The man who rented the conspirators the house in which they stored their gunpowder was John Whynniard, a Royal official. He died on the morning of 5th November, within a few hours of Guy Fawkes's arrest and no one knows how.

The catalogue of odd events in this seventeenth-century mystery goes still further. Thirty-six barrels of powder were hidden away to blow up the Houses of Parliament. Gunpowder was kept under strict control by the government, and in 1605 it was as difficult to obtain thirty-six barrels of powder as it would be now to buy thirty-six machine guns. How then did the conspirators manage to lay hands on this vast quantity of powder, and why is it that the list of stores in the Tower of London at this period, including records about gunpowder, is missing? Shreds of evidence linger on which make it appear as if the government, for some peculiar reason, was actually helping the conspirators to get their plot off the ground.

Gunpowder mystery

In December, 1605, a shrewd Italian diplomat wrote: "Those who have experience of the way in which things are done hold it as certain that there has been foul play and that some of the Council secretly spun a web to entangle these poor gentlemen (3)."

The Gunpowder Plot is a thoroughly sordid story. It is full of "the use of torture to extort signatures to convenient statements; the forgery of documents; the unscrupulous employment of propaganda; the services of the agent provocateur; the sudden deaths of vital witnesses; the art of the double-cross (4)." No modern writer of detection stories ever dreamed up a more twisted tale than that of the Gunpowder Plot. It would need a much longer book than this one to explore its blind alleys and note its red herrings, while at the end of it all the truth would still remain hidden. What you read in the following pages is therefore an attempt at a straightforward story of what probably happened.

Catholic versus Protestant

When Robert Catesby and his conspirators tried to blow up King James I and Parliament in 1605 they were not making one sudden isolated gesture. The Plot was just another phase of a continuing religious and political struggle that had begun in England some seventy years previously.

Act of Supremacy (1534)

The struggle began with the Act of Supremacy (1534) which proclaimed that Henry VIII, and not the Pope, was head of the Church in England. The Act stated: "Be it enacted by the authority of this present Parliament that the King our Sovereign Lord, his heirs and successors, kings of this realm, shall be taken, accepted and reputed the only Supreme Head in earth of the Church of England, called Anglicana Ecclesia (5)."

Henry VIII's son and successor Edward VI, who reigned from 1547–1553, held more revolutionary religious ideas than his father, and he made Protestantism the state religion. After

KING JAMES AND THE ENGLISH SUCCESSION

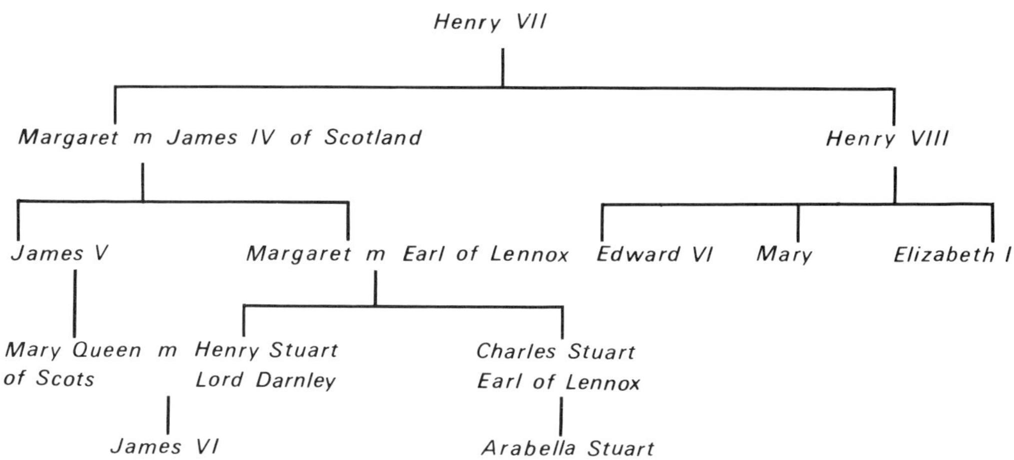

Opposite Eleven men and two women being burned at the stake. Under Mary I (1553–1558) English Protestants suffered for their faith

Overleaf Pope Pius V sends the bull excommunicating Elizabeth I

Bull of

Edward's death, his half-sister, Mary I (1553–1558), came to the throne and England swung back once again to Catholicism. Mary married King Philip II of Spain, and it was then the turn of the Protestants to suffer for their faith. "Five bishops [were burned], one and twenty divines, eight gentlemen, eighty-four artificers, an hundred husbandmen, servants and labourers, twenty-six wives, twenty widows, nine virgins, two boys and two infants. Sixty-four more were persecuted for their profession of faith; whereof seven were whipped, sixteen perished in prison, and twelve were buried in dunghills (6)."

Mary I was followed by her Protestant half-sister, Elizabeth I (1558–1603), whose Act of Supremacy (1559) confirmed Henry's law of the same name; it stated that any attempt in "writing, printing, teaching, preaching, express words, deed or act" to assert the authority of a foreign prince or prelate was treason. In 1569 the Pope retaliated, and declared Elizabeth "a heretic and abettor of heretics, and those that cleave to her in the aforesaid matters to have incurred the sentence of anathema, and to be cut off from the unity of Christ's body (7)."

Excommunication of Elizabeth I

This empty gesture by the Pope did not trouble the Queen, but it put her Catholic subjects into a terrible predicament: "And the nobles, subjects and people of the said realm and all others who have taken an oath of any kind to her, we do declare to be absolved for ever from such an oath and from all dues of dominion, fidelity, and obedience . . . and we do deprive the said Elizabeth of her pretended right to the realm . . . (8)"

Papal candidates for the throne

According to the Pope the rightful Queen of England was Mary Queen of Scots who had been expelled from her own country in favour of her infant son, James VI. Half-guest and half-prisoner in England, Mary plotted with a few Catholics who planned to release her and remove Elizabeth. The plot failed and she was executed.

The next Papal candidate for the English throne was Philip II of Spain, husband of the dead Mary Tudor. His attempt to invade England in 1588 – the famous Spanish Armada which ended disastrously with the loss of over fifty ships and twenty thousand men – represented an effort both to gain the throne of England for himself, and to reconquer the heretic realm for

Opposite Ignatius Loyola, the founder of the Society of Jesus

19

The Battle of the Spanish Armada (1588)

Catholicism. During the last years of the sixteenth century government propaganda had built up the Catholics into a community of traitors trying to disturb the peace of the land, and restore their faith with the help of foreign troops and money. They were subjected to a code of laws calculated to make their lives so unpleasant that they would either abandon their faith and become Protestants, or leave the realm.

Recusants

It was made illegal for Catholics to attend Mass, and in 1581 it became high treason, punishable by death, to attempt to convert anyone to Catholicism. A "Recusant", which was the

name given to anyone who did not attend the services of the Church of England, was first punished by having to pay a fine of one shilling per week, but later the penalty rose to a massive twenty pounds per month. Also, anyone who helped or harboured priests could be charged by the government with treason.

The Jesuits

The government intensified its attacks on the Catholic priests because it considered, rightly, that they held the English Catholic community together, and prevented it from crumbling. The priests the government feared and hated most of all were those

Overleaf During Elizabeth I's reign, Catholics were put to death for their beliefs

who belonged to the Society of Jesus. This religious order had been founded in 1540 by Ignatius Loyola, who was formerly an officer in the Spanish army. It was concerned mainly with missionary work, and Ignatius knew exactly the sort of men that he wanted for dangerous and challenging jobs in hostile lands: "He who is no good in the world is certainly no good in the Society either (9)."

The government maintained a continual propaganda campaign against the young Englishmen who were trained in the Jesuit college at Douai in France, and then returned secretly to support the Catholic community. One report by a Jesuit said: "There is tremendous talk here of Jesuits and more fables perhaps are told about them than were told of old about monsters. For as to the origin of these men, their way of life, their institute, their morals and teaching, their plans and actions, stories of all sorts are spread abroad, not only in private conversations, but also in public sermons and printed books, and these contradict one another and have a striking resemblance to dreams (10)."

Another account from a Jesuit stated that "heretics seek to make the very name Jesuit a bug-bear . . . We are called the Pope's Janissaries, the favourite brood of Antichrist, the sworn slaves of the Pope. They say that Hell hath sent us forth fully equipped (11)."

Pursuivants

These Jesuit priests were in the forefront when it came to sustaining the morale of the English Catholics who were suffering greatly from the penal laws that had been imposed on them. There were also tribes of legalized bandits called "pursuivants" who had come into being to enforce these laws. Here is a description of a typical pursuivants' raid: "What a thing it is for a Catholic gentleman to have his house suddenly beset on all sides with a number of men in arms, both horse and foot, and not only his house and garden . . . but all highways laid for some miles near unto him, that none shall pass but they shall be examined. Then are these searchers so rude and barbarous that, if the doors be not opened in the instant when they would enter, they break open all the doors with all violence, as if they were to sack a town of enemies won by the sword . . .

"The searchers being thus entered it hath been usual with pursuivants to run up the stairs and into the chambers with their drawn swords, enough to drive the weaker sort of women and children out of their wits. Then they begin to break off locks and open all the doors of the house presently, that they may at one time search in many places. Then if they find no priest nor suspected persons . . . they go presently to search for secret places . . .

"Sometimes, if the walls be not made of stone, but of wainscot or other weak matter, they will thrust through it with their swords in many places, hoping that in some place or other they will light upon a priest. . . . They then break down the walls wholly and enter themselves to search with candles and torches in all such dark places and in housetops where sometimes nothing but mice or birds have come for many years . . . When the searchers find not any priest for all this cruel diligence they have used, yet will they not give over, but supposing there is or may be some so secretly hidden . . . Then they appoint a watch about the house and every part thereof fifty or sixty men . . .

"Sometimes also they place watchmen in the chambers of the house within . . . When they can find no priest, which they chiefly desire to take in any man's house because then his lands and goods and life also are forfeited . . . they break open chests and trunks; then to cabinets and little boxes for letters, hoping to find some spiritual advice in them . . . thereby to infer that they are priests' letters with whom they have acquaintance; or if they find any Agnus Deis or beads or medals that they can prove are hallowed, then also all the lands and goods of the parties are seized and themselves condemned to perpetual imprisonment (12)."

In circumstances such as these it is not surprising that the Catholics became desperate. Their hope was that when old Elizabeth died her successor might show at least a little more mercy to their religion.

2 Catholic Fears

The new King

ELIZABETH I's successor to the throne of England was King James I (1603–1625). He was the son of Mary Queen of Scots, and – when Elizabeth died in 1603 – he was already reigning as King James VI of Scotland. By the age of thirty-seven "he was of middling stature, more corpulent through his clothes than in his body, yet fat enough, his clothes being made large and easy, the doublets quilted for stiletto proof, his breeches in great pleats and full stuffed. He was naturally of a timorous disposition, which was the reason for his quilted doublets. His eyes large, ever rolling after a stranger that came into his presence, insomuch as many have left the room as being out of countenance. His beard was very thin, his tongue too large for his mouth, which ever made him speak full in the mouth, and made him drink very uncomely . . . His walk was ever circular, his fingers ever in that walk fiddling about his cod piece (13)."

It was inconceivable to Catholics throughout England that James could ever be as harsh a tyrant to them as Queen Elizabeth had been: "Most Catholics had great hope and expectation of this king . . . First they did and might expect that the son of such a mother, who not only lived as a Catholic in her kingdom and in prison but died also because she was a Catholic, would himself also be a friend to Catholics at least, if he would not be a follower of the Catholic religion (14)." In fact, not only was James the son of a Catholic queen but his wife, Anne of Denmark, was of the same faith.

Besides emotional reasons for James favouring the Catholics, there were other practical circumstances which could have

Opposite The coronation of James I of England

James I of England (1603–1625) with his son, Charles

induced him to tolerate the Catholics rather than the Protestants. In Catholic eyes Elizabeth I had never been a true Queen of England. This was because she was illegitimate – the daughter of Henry VIII and Ann Boleyn, whom the Pope failed to recognize as a lawful wife. So far as the Pope was concerned, however, James VI of Scotland was also, legitimately, James I of England.

James's tolerant nature

But when James reigned as King of Scotland he occasionally expressed opinions that promised a naturally tolerant attitude to religion: "I did ever hold persecution as one of the infallible notes of a false church (15)," he said. On another occasion he avowed: "I will never agree that any man should die for errors of faith (16)."

James's need of Catholic support

There was also a sound political reason why James needed the active goodwill and support of the Catholics. Although his claim to the throne was good he was not the only one in line.

Arabella Stuart (1575–1615), an English-born descendant of Henry VII

Arabella Stuart, an English-born descendant of Henry VII, was a contender, and the nobles who preferred her as sovereign might try to enlist Catholic sympathy.

In 1603, as soon as it became apparent that old Queen Elizabeth was about to die, James received a messenger named Thomas Percy, who brought advice from the Earl of Northumberland that Catholic assistance could be bought for a modest price. The Earl's family was traditionally Catholic and his support of the comparatively new Church of England was only skin deep. His message read: "It were a pity to lose so good a kingdom for the not tolerating Mass in a corner, if upon that it resteth, so long as they shall not be too busy disturbers of the government of the state, nor seek to make us contribute to a Peter priest (17)." James' reply spoke well for the Catholics: "I will neither persecute any that will be quiet and give but an outward obedience to the law; neither will I spare to advance any of them that will by good service worthily deserve it (18)."

Catholic optimism

After Queen Elizabeth's death James began to prepare for his journey to England. All Catholics were full of optimism: "Everyone who comes here from Scotland affirms that the religion of this country will not be changed, except that the recusant Catholics who have agreed to pay to the Crown a large sum of money every month in lieu of attendance at heretical services may perhaps be relieved of that payment and freed from persecution for their religious acts in private (19)."

And the hopes of the Catholics in England were matched by those of the Pope in Rome: "His Holiness here is so far embarked to try what may be done by fair means with him, as until the contrary do appear by manifest proofs and that it be confirmed also by sufficient time, he will harken to nothing against him (20)."

However, as soon as James was secure on the throne of England many of his attitudes changed. He realized that if he showed leniency to his Catholic subjects he would lose the support of the non-Catholic majority. So, Parliament was allowed to pass a law providing that all Elizabeth's laws "against any manner of recusants shall be put into due and exact execution."

The result of this move was that a mentally unstable Catholic priest, named William Watson, who was "a very short man, very purblind, looketh asquint" devised a fatuous plot to kidnap the King. The plot failed, largely because it was revealed to the King by the Jesuits. James showed his gratitude to them by suspending the recusancy fines.

Catholic revival

A Catholic revival in England followed. Many people who had said they belonged to the established Anglican Church now showed where their true sympathies lay and rejoined the Church of their fathers. One report said of the Catholics: "It is hardly credible in what jollity they now live. They make no question to obtain at least a toleration if not an alteration in religion; in hope whereof many who did dutifully frequent the Church are of late become recusants (21)."

Robert Cecil, who was the Secretary of State, was warned by his brother that "the infection of Popery does so spread abroad as many that held clear before begin to decline . . . It must be looked to in time (22)."

Robert Cecil

Robert Cecil was then about forty years old, and his position meant that he was the King's chief adviser. He was a limping, sick, round-shouldered little man of great intelligence and industry. He found it impossible to be frank and honest, and was without true friends. James heaped titles on him – Baron Cecil of Essendon, Viscount Cranborne and Earl of Salisbury. He also loaded him with cruel nicknames based on the Secretary's odd appearance. Cecil himself said: "I see nothing that I can do can procure me so much favour as to be sure one whole day what title I shall have another. For from Essendon to Cranborne, from Cranborne to Salisbury, from Salisbury to 'Beagle', from 'Beagle' to 'Tom Derry'" – or Tom Thumb as we would say – "from 'Tom Derry' to 'Parrot', which I hate most, I have been walked (23)."

This was the man who was advised that the rising tide of Catholicism must be "looked to." Almost certainly it was his insistent and cunning pressure upon James that brought the King's honeymoon with the Catholics to an abrupt close in February, 1605.

It became clear that there was no future in England for the

Destroying Catholicism

Catholics. Even if their religious beliefs were not suspected, the political position of the Pope was. The Venetian Ambassador sounded Cecil out on the whole matter: "I asked him what was the cause of this extraordinary movement against the Catholics, for I could see no reason which justified the persecution. He [Cecil] replied, 'The King's excessive clemency has ended in this, that priests go openly about the country, the city, and private houses, saying mass, and this gives great offence to others.' "

When the Ambassador continued to protest, Cecil, usually so smooth, responded brutally: " 'It cannot be helped; there are laws, and they must be observed, and there is no doubt that the object of these laws is to extinguish the Catholic religion in this kingdom; for we hold it undesirable in a well governed monarchy to allow the increase of persons who profess obedience to the will of a foreign sovereign as the Catholics do . . . If the world can be assured that the Papal superiority will be confined exclusively to affairs spiritual – this point once established I assure you that the next day the King would concede liberty of conscience and permit the exercise of the Catholic religion, but on no other terms can it be thought of (24).' "

Robert Catesby

One Catholic gentleman who despaired of any worthwhile improvement for his fellow Catholics under the existing order of things was Robert Catesby. He was thirty-two years old, and comfortably off with estates in the Midlands, a house at Uxbridge, and rented apartments in the Strand, the fashionable part of London. Catesby had come to the unfavourable attention of the authorities once, when he had supported the Earl of Essex in a wild attempt to overthrow Elizabeth I's ministers, and particularly Robert Cecil. One of the reasons why he had sided with Essex was that the Earl seemed to promise toleration for the Catholics.

John Gerard, a Jesuit priest who knew all the conspirators, said: "Mr. Catesby, who as it seems by many circumstances was the first inventor and chiefest furtherer of the plot, was a gentleman of an ancient and great family in England, whose chief estate was in Warwickshire . . . [As a young man] he was very wild . . . so he spent much above his rate, and so wasted also a

Robert Catesby, the leading conspirator in the Gunpowder Plot

good part of his living. Some four or five years before Queen Elizabeth died he was reclaimed from his wild courses, and became a Catholic. After this he left his swearing and excess of play and apparel and all wild company . . .

"About three years before the Queen's death, when the Earl of Essex did intend and attempt by force to put down some of those that ruled the state . . . Mr. Catesby was a principal man in the action, having first received a faithful promise from the Earl of toleration at least for all Catholics . . . Mr. Catesby did show such valour and fought so long and stoutly as afterwards divers of those swordsmen did exceedingly esteem him . . . He was very wise and of great judgement, though his utterance not so good. He was so liberal and apt to help all sorts, as it got him much love. He was of person about two yards high and, though slender, yet as well proportioned to his height as any man one should see (25)."

There can be no doubt that Robert Catesby brooded long and hard over the condition of the English Catholics before he requested the help of Thomas Percy and John Wright, two friends, both of whom were members like himself of the unsuccessful Essex rebellion. Percy it must be remembered had carried the Earl of Northumberland's message advising toleration for Catholics to James while he was still only King of Scotland.

Thomas Percy

"Mr. Thomas Percy was of the name and kindred of one of the ancientest and greatest Earls in England . . . His estate was not great, depending most upon the said Earl . . . under whom he had the keeping of a castle and the receiving of his rents, with the overlooking and command of his tenants in those parts . . . For the most part of his youth he had been very wild, more than ordinary, and much given to fighting, so that it was noted in him and Mr. John Wright, whose sister he afterwards married, that if they heard of any man in the country to be esteemed more valiant and resolute than others, one or the other of them would surely have picked some quarrel against him and fought with him to have made trial of his valour."

Percy had become a Catholic about the time of the Essex rising, yet despite his conversion – and perhaps because he was related to the great Earl of Northumberland – he obtained a position under King James's Crown: "Living for the most part in London . . . he was made one of the Gentlemen Pensioners in Ordinary." He was about forty-five years old, powerfully built, with greying hair and beard, and "had a great wit, and a very good delivery of his mind (26)."

John Wright

Catesby's other associate, John Wright, "was a gentleman of Yorkshire, not born to any great fortune, but lived always in place and company of the better sort. In youth and for the most part of his time very wild and disposed to fighting . . . He became a Catholic about the time of Lord Essex's attempt, in which he was." Although he relished action, Wright was not just a hot-head and Catesby admired "his valour and secrecy in carriage of any business (27)."

Catesby must have approached Percy and Wright towards the end of 1603 and having won their approval, with what amount of persuasion no one knows, he felt safe to draw in more people to the Plot. The next man he approached was Thomas Winter.

Thomas Winter

Thomas Winter was born in 1565 and "was a younger brother of the house of Huddington in the county of Worcester . . . This gentleman had spent his youth well, for he was a reasonable good scholar and able to talk in many matters of learning, but especially in philosophies or history very well and judiciously. He could speak both Latin, Italian, Spanish and French. He had been a soldier both in Flanders, France and against the Turk and could discourse exceeding well of these matters. And he was of such a wit, and so fine carriage that he was of so pleasing conversation, desired much of the better sort, but an inseparable friend to Mr. Robert Catesby. He was of mean stature, but strong and comely and very valiant (28)."

Winter is important not only for what he did in the Plot, but because his confession, which he made after the Plot had been discovered, was one of the two that were published.

According to Winter's confession, he received a message from Catesby suggesting that they should meet in London. Although this invitation was from his "inseparable friend," Winter refused. He was ill, depressed, and considering leaving England in order to join the Catholic exiles in Flanders. However, he was soon to receive a further letter from Catesby: "Shortly I received another letter, in any wise to come. I presently came up, and found him with Mr. John Wright at Lambeth, where he broke with me, how necessary it was not to foresake our country . . . but to deliver her from the servitude in which she remained (29)."

Catesby's plan

Then Catesby came to the point: "He said that he had bethought him of a way at one instant to deliver us from all our bonds, and without any foreign help to replant again the Catholic religion; and withal told me in a word, it was to blow up the Parliament-house with gunpowder; for said he, in that place have they done us all the mischief, and perchance God hath designed that place for their punishment (30)."

Winter, who was a scholar, soldier and traveller, was not to be stampeded into rash action. His confession does not reveal whether he made any moral objections to Catesby's plot, but the fact that it could have disastrous political consequences is certainly pointed out: "If it should not take effect, as most of this nature miscarried, the scandal would be so great . . . as not only our enemies but our friends also would condemn us (31)."

Catesby had lost faith in half-measures, and saw a policy of all-or-nothing as the only one that might help the Catholics. He made no attempt to mince his words. If Parliament was to be blown up it was because "the nature of the disease requires so sharp a remedy (32)."

One very slim chance remained that it might be possible to win toleration for Catholicism without resorting to gunpowder. By this time the long drawn-out war between England and Spain had come to a standstill, and formal peace terms were being negotiated. The King of Spain's representative, the Constable of Castile, was based in Brussels, and as part of the overall peace settlement he might have been able to request a greater degree of toleration for the English Catholics. But it would have been an unlikely chance as one of the charges brought against the English Catholics was that their religion united them with England's foe, Spain. Nevertheless, if anyone had the ability to enlist the Constable's help it was the well-travelled and scholarly Winter.

In his instructions to Winter Catesby said: "Because we will leave no peaceable and quiet way untried you shall go over and inform the Constable of the state of the Catholics here in England, entreating him to solicit his Majesty at his coming hither, that the penal laws may be recalled, and we admitted into the ranks of his other subjects (33)."

Even as he issued these instructions Catesby must have doubted what they would achieve, for he also ordered Winter to enlist "some confident gentlemen, such as you shall understand best able for this business (34)."

Guy Fawkes

There were at the time plenty of English Catholics in Flanders – especially in Sir William Stanley's regiment which was in Spanish service. Among those in the regiment whom Catesby requested Winter to contact was a school fellow of John Wright named Guy Fawkes. Fawkes was born in York in 1570, and had been on a mission to Spain, either as a diplomat or as a courier. He was described as tall, with brown hair and an auburn beard, "a man of great piety, of exemplary temperance, of mild and cheerful demeanour, an enemy of broils and disputes (35)."

When Winter returned to England with Fawkes he knew that international diplomacy would not help the English Catholics. He replied tersely when Catesby asked him about the Constable of Castile's reception: "Good words, but I fear the deeds will not match (36)." It was obvious that the English Catholics would have to stand or fall by their own resources.

The mission to Flanders convinced Winter, who was by nature a cool man, that the only solution to the problem lay in action. Thomas Percy, although an older man, felt the same way but was more impatient. His first words when he next met Catesby and the other conspirators were: "Shall we always, gentlemen, talk and never do anything? (37)" Catesby calmed him down, but a few days later the group re-assembled to develop their plan, and to take an oath of secrecy. Robert Catesby, Thomas Percy, John Wright, Thomas Winter and Guy Fawkes had launched what was to become "The Gunpowder Treason."

After the meeting the conspirators got down to practicalities. Their objective was to blow up the Lords' Chamber in the Houses of Parliament at the very moment when King James

Guy Fawkes, the conspirator chosen to blow up the Lords' Chamber in the Houses of Parliament

was opening a new session, and the great majority of Lords and Commons would be present to hear him read his speech. At the beginning of the seventeenth century the Houses of Parliament were not as they are now. They were a complex of buildings in the approximate form of an "H". The Lords' Chamber was at the bridge of the H, and the conspirators leased a house in the lower left-hand leg of the H, which belonged to John Whynniard, Keeper of the Wardrobe. The plan was to tunnel from this house to a point beneath the bridge of the H, where they would excavate a cavity, in which they would pile barrels of gunpowder. Even when this powder was placed it would not be directly beneath the room in which James would deliver his speech.

The House of Lords was a two-storey building; the first floor – odd though this may seem by modern standards – was hired out to a coal merchant called Bright. The powder was therefore to be beneath this ground-level store room.

Whynniard's house had been rented by Thomas Percy, and Guy Fawkes, under the assumed name of John Johnson, was appointed caretaker. The conspirators also needed a storage point, where they "might make provision of powder and wood for the mine, which being there ready should in a night be conveyed by boat to the house by the Parliament (38)." The obvious choice was the house in Lambeth which Robert Catesby used, and to keep an eye on this side of the operation another man named Robert Keyes was brought into the conspiracy.

Robert Keyes

Keyes came from Northamptonshire and Catholic evidence describes him as "a grave and sober man." This, however, is hard to credit as another report of his behaviour at his brother-in-law's house sums up a very different person: "He suddenly whipped out his sword and in merriment made many offers therewith at the heads, necks, and sides of several gentlemen and ladies." People who indulge in horseplay with lethal weapons should be distrusted, but this dangerous capering was "taken for a mere frolic." Afterwards, when the plot was discovered, "such as remembered his gestures thought he practised what he intended to do when the Plot should take effect (39)."

The house in Lambeth where the conspirators stored the gunpowder

The tunnelling, or mining as the conspirators called it, began about 11th December, 1604: "We all five entered with tools fit to begin our work having provided ourselves of baked meats, the less to need sending abroad. We entered late in the night, and we never saw [anyone], save only Mr. Percy's man, until Christmas Eve. In which time we wrought under a little entry to the wall of the Parliament-house, and underpropped it, as we went, with wood (40)." According to Fawkes, he and the rest of the miners "had shot and powder, being resolved to die in that place, before we should yield or be taken (41)."

There are some inconsistencies in the stories of Winter and Fawkes, about how far and fast they dug, but these are points of no great importance. The foundation wall of Parliament, "which was about three yards thick . . . and a matter of great difficulty (42)," must have daunted them. It was wretched work tunnelling in the "Vault of Villainy," since none of them was used to manual labour and two of them were uncommonly tall men. They rested over Christmas, and then transferred all their powder barrels from Catesby's house, across the River Thames, to the Whynniard property.

And then, as they dug, a stroke of luck occurred, although at first it seemed like impending discovery and doom. Guy Fawkes recounts: "While they [the miners] were a-working upon the wall they heard a rushing in the cellar of removing of coals, whereupon we feared we had been discovered, and they sent me to the cellar." He found "that the coals were a-selling, and that the cellar was to be let . . . Percy [then] went and hired the same for a yearly rent (43)." In fact, what they had acquired was not a cellar at all, but the large ground floor room immediately below the Lords' Chamber.

At this stage it is time to introduce one of those red herrings in which the story of the Gunpowder Plot is so very rich. It has been asked – and no satisfactory answer has ever been given – whether there was a tunnel at all. Although one confession by Guy Fawkes was printed, he was interrogated many times, and it was only on the fifth occasion that he mentioned the tunnel. But setting aside that strange fact, there are some odd practical questions to consider. What did the conspirators do with the vast quantities of stone and earth that they are supposed to have excavated? It will not do to say that they used it to raise the level of the nearest garden, or that they carried it down to the River Thames at dead of night.

But, if, for the sake of argument, we accept that they did dispose of the rubble in this way, it is most peculiar that no one heard them digging. There was plenty of activity around the

Houses of Parliament, even when they were not in session, and people lived close by. With all these considerations in mind, would the conspirators have been foolhardy enough to attempt tunnelling? If they were so rash it is a miracle that they were not discovered, and to this "miracle" we shall eventually return.

Yet, if there was no mine, what was the government's motive in inventing one? Robert Cecil was far too economic by temperament to circulate a wholly pointless lie. The explanation could be that there were genuine circumstances about the Plot that he did not wish to become subjects for popular gossip. By confusing the issue with tall stories about "mines" and "Vaults of Villainy" he expected to divert public attention from these other matters.

The conspirators' plans

The conspirators were not simple souls who thought that the mere act of removing the King and some of his councillors would be sufficient to usher in a new golden age for the Catholics of England. They knew that they had to think in terms of an alternative government, and it seems a foregone conclusion that Catesby would have outlined some proposals when he first broached the idea of blowing up Parliament to his friends.

The King's children

Yet, according to Winter's statement, which must be distorted and edited in this matter, the conspirators only began to develop their plans as they dug: "The first question was, how we might surprise the next heir; the prince [of Wales] would haply be at the Parliament with the King, his father; how should we then be able to seize the Duke? [Charles] (44)."

With Henry, Prince of Wales, blown sky-high, young Duke Charles – who later became Charles I and was then five years old – was a trump card in the conspirators' game. As Thomas Percy was a Gentleman Pensioner in Ordinary he had considerable freedom in moving about the Royal households, so he "with another gentleman would enter the chamber without suspicion; and having some dozen others at several doors to expect his coming and two or three on horseback to receive him, he would undertake . . . to carry him safe away (45)."

According to Fawkes, however, the plans for Charles were different: "We had sundry consultations on how to seize his person, but because we found no means how to encompass it, the Duke being kept near London, where we had not forces

Opposite The cellar below the Lords' Chamber

Guy Fawkes and Robert Catesby taking gunpowder from Lambeth to Westminster, across the River Thames

enough, we resolved to serve our turn with the Lady Elizabeth (46)."

James's daughter, the Princess Elizabeth, was then nine years old and in the care of Lord Harington at Combe Abbey in Warwickshire. Thomas Winter commented: "It were easy to surprise her in the country, by drawing friends together at a hunting near the Lord Harington's, and Ashby, Mr. Catesby's house, being not far off, was a fit place for preparation (47)."

Saving the Lords

The next question the conspirators had to decide was what Lords should be saved from the Parliament. Not all those present were persecutors of the Catholics. Some were Catholics themselves, some were well disposed, and others were related to Catholics. At the time the simple answer was they would somehow preserve "as many as we could that were Catholics or so disposed (48)." Later on, there was to be some hard talking among the conspirators on this score.

No foreign involvement

Because France and Spain were Catholic powers with fleets and armies, and because the Pope was also a temporal ruler, it was natural to wonder whether they could play a useful part in restoring Catholicism to England. The conspirators had to think of "what foreign princes we should acquaint with this plot before or join with after (49)." Remembering Winter's mission to the Constable of Castile and the subsequent disappointment they did not linger too long on that topic. "We agreed that first we could not enjoin princes to that secrecy . . . so as to be secure of their promise; besides, we knew not whether they will approve the project or dislike it (50)."

In short what emerged from these conversations in the mine – which we shall assume were elaborated and developed there, but begun in more comfortable surroundings – was a complete plan for an illegal change of government. It was arranged that Guy Fawkes should blow up Parliament, thus killing James, the Prince of Wales, Robert Cecil, members of the Privy Council and many others besides, so that the country would be virtually without a central government. Some of the conspirators were to seize, at least, Princess Elizabeth, and perhaps Duke Charles.

The full conspiracy

Robert Catesby would operate in London to stir up embers of resentment against the dead King. He would remind everyone

The conspirators' meeting at a house in the Strand

of the King's intentions to unite England and Scotland – the idea most Londoners detested. There was a very reasonable hope that once the King was dead and the conspirators had an alternative monarch – either Elizabeth or Charles – to rally to, the strongly Catholic counties in the North, the Midlands, and Wales might rise in arms. Finally, although foreign powers could not be relied upon, it was possible that Sir William Stanley's regiment of English Catholics might land on the south coast.

3 *The Cellars of Westminster*

More resources needed

THIS AMBITIOUS PLAN to blow up the Lords' Chamber in the Houses of Parliament could not be carried out exclusively by the little band sweating away below ground. It needed far more men, more operational bases, and considerably more money for it to work. One of the conspirators describes how it became necessary for Robert Catesby to call in other members to the Plot so as to spread the costs: "By reason that the charge of maintaining us all so long together, besides the number of several houses which for several uses had been hired, and buying of powder *et cetera*, had lain heavy on Mr. Catesby alone to support, it was necessary for him to call in some others to ease his charge (51)."

Among the most spectacular of the new recruits was the youthful Sir Everard Digby, "one of the chiefest men of Rutlandshire." He was a convert to Catholicism, who joined the conspirators for "the friendship and love he bare to Catesby, which prevailed so much and was so powerful with him as that for his sake he was ever contented and ready to hazard himself and his estate (52)."

Digby was clearly a remarkable young man in every respect: "Of stature about two yards high, very little lower than Mr. Catesby, but of stronger making. Very cunning at his weapon, much practised and expert in riding of great horses, of which he kept divers in his stable continually . . . He was a good musician and kept divers good musicians in his house." He was also skilled in indoor games, presumably chess and the like, "which are usual for gentlemen in foul weather when they are forced to keep house (53)."

The Catholic priest, whose accounts of the plotters were naturally biased, said: "I have heard many say that they had not seen the like of a young man [Digby], and that his carriage and manner of discourse were more like to a grave councillor of State than to a gallant of the court as he was, and a man but of twenty-six years old (54)."

Sir Everard Digby

Ambrose Rookwood

Digby's athleticism, interests, property and wealth were all to be put to use for the Plot. As a strong young swordsman he was a natural leader to organize the rising of the Midland Catholics. As a well-known sportsman he could assemble a large number of well-mounted men, "as it were to a match of hunting which he had made," without arousing suspicion. These men would then make a dash to capture Princess Elizabeth.

As a base for his operations Digby hired a house at Coughton, near Stratford-on-Avon. This was within easy striking distance of Dunsmore Heath, the rendezvous for the hunting match, which in turn was half a dozen miles from Combe Abbey, where Princess Elizabeth lived. He was also able to afford a contribution of £1,500 towards the conspirators' general funds.

Another similar person to Digby was Ambrose Rookwood, a twenty-six year old gentleman of considerable wealth who lived at Coldham Hall near Bury St. Edmunds. Like Digby he joined the conspiracy primarily for the sake of Robert Catesby, whom he "esteemed dearer than anything else in the world (55)." The conspirators wanted Rookwood "not so much to have his help by his living [*i.e.* his money] as by his person, and

Ambrose Rookwood

John Grant

Father Henry Garnet

some provision of horses, of which he had divers of the best (56)." He was obviously the sort of person who could be expected to go to a hunting match with a string of fast-striding horses and a band of sturdy companions without it exciting too much comment. Although it is said that his cash resources were not important, the conspirators must have been pleased that he could afford to rent an additional Midlands base. This was Clopton Hall near Stratford-on-Avon which was close to the home of yet another new conspirator, John Grant.

John Grant

Grant was a native of Warwickshire, and just the type for the desperate venture that Catesby was organizing: "He was as fierce as a lion," and when pursuivants came to his house looking for priests, "he paid them so well for their labour not with crowns of gold but with cracked crowns sometimes, and with dry blows instead of drink . . . His mettle and manner of proceeding was so well known unto them that it kept them very much in awe, and himself in much quiet, which he did the rather use, that he might with more safety keep a priest in his house (57)." Another Midlander who was also won over into the conspiracy was Thomas Winter's elder brother Robert, who lived at Huddington Hall.

Francis Tresham

Francis Tresham, "a gentleman of Northamptonshire of great estate," who had been involved in the Earl of Essex's rebellion joined the conspirators, too. His father Sir Thomas, who had been among the English Catholics who gave King James I a loyal welcome on his accession, had just died, and Francis was very rich. He promised the conspiracy £2,000. However, he seems to have not been so dedicated as the other conspirators. "This gentleman had been wild in his youth and even till his end was not known to be of so good example as the rest . . . It is thought by most that Mr. Tresham had not that zeal for the advancement of the Catholics' cause . . . as the others had (58)."

Lord Monteagle

It is important to notice that Tresham's sister was the wife of a certain Lord Monteagle, who had been a Catholic, but who joined the Church of England when James came to the throne. Monteagle rose quickly in James's favour and yet, remarkably enough, he was also on close terms with all the conspirators. He was in touch, too, with a number of Jesuit priests, including the Superior of the English Jesuits, Father Henry Garnet.

Thomas Bates

If Tresham was the odd man out in terms of character and integrity, the conspirators also acquired an odd man out in terms of social class. So far, all of them were "gentlemen" in the seventeenth-century sense of the word – that is, landowners who knew and were proud of their ancestry. Now they were joined by Thomas Bates, who was certainly not a poor man but was a member of Catesby's household. Bates became united with the conspirators after Catesby had noticed "that his man observed him extraordinarily . . . [so he] called him to him . . . and . . . asked him what he thought the business was they went about . . . He answered that he thought they intended some dangerous matter about the Parliament-house, because he had been sent to get a lodging near unto that place. Then they did make the said Bates take an oath to be secret in the action (59)."

At the same time as new men were being enlisted to help, the original conspirators were also taking stock of needs and resources. Percy, for example, promised "all he could get out of the Earl of Northumberland's rents" which was about £4,000, and to provide "many galloping horses."

When Thomas Winter had first been approached by Robert Catesby, he had some doubts about the Plot. Later, as the conspirators worked in the mine, they had talked about ways to ensure that Catholic lords, and lords who were friendly to the Catholics, should not be killed when Parliament was blown up. Now it was the turn of Ambrose Rookwood to ask Catesby whether this mass assassination was permissible.

He first wanted to know "how such as were Catholics and divers other friends should be preserved." Catesby replied, rather vaguely, that "there should be a trick put upon them." Rookwood was not satisfied, and pointed out that "it was a matter of conscience to take away so much blood." At this point Catesby changed his mind. Having first said that the Catholic lords and others would be saved "by a trick" he suddenly said that he was "in conscience resolved that it might be done (60)." In other words, even if no lords were saved, their death would not be a crime.

Catesby and Father Garnet

Catesby also told Rookwood that he had come to this conclusion after discussions with Father Henry Garnet, the Superior of the English Jesuits. He had not admitted the existence of the Gunpowder Plot to any, but "had put the like case, and he was resolved by good authority that it be done . . . He had also asked advice whether if it could not be done without the destruction of some innocents whether the act might be done. And he was resolved that, rather than the action should fail, they must also suffer as the rest did (61)."

Unfortunately, in his anxiety to ensure the support of the scrupulous Rookwood, Catesby was not being strictly honest. He had indeed talked with Garnet during the summer, but it was not about whether the assassination of the lords was permissible, or anything like it. He had led Garnet to suppose that he was going over to Flanders to command a regiment of English Catholics there. Therefore he was interested in the moral position of a soldier who, in the normal course of war, might be responsible for the death of innocent non-combatants. Garnet suggested that, in certain conditions, a soldier might be excused or forgiven if he was indirectly responsible for the deaths of such people.

Later, however, Garnet was adamant that Catesby had never mentioned the Plot to him: "Mr. Catesby nor none of the other conspirators ever propounded the case to me . . . only Mr. Catesby asked whether if one intended lawfully to kill any man he might do it, notwithstanding the hazards of innocents. I, nothing imagining either the King's person or any such horrible massacre as this, answered that oftentimes in wars such things were done, so that they were such as the victory might countervail the innocents' death (62)." He added that he had thought Catesby's question was purely theoretical: "Neither did I then think that it was a question to be put into practice . . . Generally I thought all insurrection against the King unlawful (63)."

Garnet's suspicions

But Garnet's position was not quite as straightforward as he stated. In the summer of 1604, a whole year before this talk about the massacre of the innocent lords, he had written a nervous letter to the Superior of the Jesuits in Rome. He had understood from "some friends that Mr. Catesby was much missing from the places where he was wont to resort continually for spiritual help; and hearing also, that he and other gentlemen of forward humour did keep much together and had many secret meetings, he began to suspect that they had something in hand (64)."

This was before the Constable of Castile came to England to confirm the peace treaty between England and Spain, at which time it was hoped he would persuade James I to relax the persecution of the Catholics. If he did not succeed, Garnet saw dangerous consequences, and he added a footnote to his letter, in code: "If the affair of toleration go not well, Catholics will no more be quiet. What shall we do? Jesuits cannot hinder it. Let Pope forbid all Catholics to stir (65)." With fears and suspicions like this in his mind it is strange that Garnet did not connect Catesby's behaviour in the summer of 1605 with the strange questions that he had previously asked.

Catesby admits Plot

Although Garnet never heard about the Plot from Catesby he did become aware of it. In July, 1605, during confession to the Jesuit, Father Oswald Tesimond, Catesby admitted the Plot. Possibly he had a pang of conscience about the way he had wheedled Garnet into saying something that could be loosely interpreted as a pardon for blowing up innocent people. In any event, he agreed that when Tesimond in turn confessed to Father Garnet, he might reveal to him what he knew of the Plot.

The secrecy of the Catholic confessional is total. No priest may disclose anything he hears at confession to a third person unless the penitent agrees. In addition, a priest is not allowed to raise any matter outside the confessional box that has been discussed within it, unless the penitent agrees.

So when Garnet learned, through Tesimond, of "this most horrible thing, the like of which was never heard of, for many reasons unlawful (66)," he could not try to dissuade Catesby from it, because it was something that he had heard through the secrecy of the confessional. It was evident to him that a horrible tragedy was in the making, which he could not directly prevent.

The only way around his predicament was to write again to the Superior in Rome, disclosing nothing, but making discreet suggestions based on what he knew. "The danger is lest secretly some treason of violence be shown to the King, and so all Catholics may be compelled to take arms. Wherefore in my judgement two things are necessary; first, that his Holiness should prescribe what in any case is to be done, and then that he should forbid any force of arms to the Catholics under censures (67)."

Garnet was doing whatever he could to prevent the Plot developing – within the limits imposed upon him as a priest, by the rules of the Catholic religion. It is clear, though, that a hostile government that did not recognize the secrecy of the confessional, could accuse him of being an accomplice in the Plot because he did not reveal it. In fact, the government was to do more. The claim was later put out that Garnet was the originator of the Plot. This was a valuable point in the propaganda war against the hated Jesuits.

Plan goes ahead

Throughout the summer of 1605 the conspirators pushed ahead with their plans. Ambrose Rookwood and John and Christopher Wright moved into the Midlands, John Grant bought fifty new muskets, three suits of armour, and eight barrels of gunpowder, and concealed them for use in the Midland rebellion. To show that they were crusaders at heart, Thomas Winter, Ambrose Rookwood, and Christopher Wright ordered new swords whose hilts were engraved with Christ's passion. And Guy Fawkes laid in a fresh supply of powder, and more wood beneath which to hide it.

Events outside the conspirators' control must have given them cause to expect that the Midland rising would succeed. On Ash Wednesday, 1605, the King harangued his Council against the Catholics, "protesting his utter detestation of their superstitious religion" and asserting that "if he thought that his son and heir would give any toleration thereunto, he would wish him fairly buried before his eyes (68)." He gave the judges "a very straight charge to be diligent and severe in their circuits against recusants and to execute the laws in that behalf made." As a result of his encouragement the judges imposed heavy fines and Garnet wrote that "the courses taken are more severe than in Queen Elizabeth's time (69)."

Catholics become militant

The Catholics did not take this persecution meekly. Reports came in to Robert Cecil of their militant mood. The Bishop of Hereford was particularly alarmed by the trend of events: "The number of recusants near this city is incredibly increased within three years. They are grown to boldness to take up weapons . . . Last Sunday three hundred were at Mass strongly armed; on Monday and Tuesday a great part of them continued, waiting for my coming (70)."

And the Bishop of Chester was equally worried: "Upon the decease of the late Queen Elizabeth, much provision was made by the recusants in these parts of armour and warlike habiliments which still remain among them (71)." This was just the warlike sort of attitude that would help Catesby and the con-

Overleaf Lord Monteagle receives the letter warning him of the Gunpowder Plot

Francis Tresham – one of the plotters and brother-in-law of Lord Monteagle

spirators when they raised the flag of Catholic rebellion.

Cecil's knowledge of the Plot

Robert Cecil was of course interested in these developments, but we can be sure that his main attention was focused elsewhere. The development which he watched most closely was that of the Gunpowder Plot itself. For Cecil, the ace spy-master, already knew of its existence. As early as April, 1604, one of his agents in Brussels, a man named Henry Wright, had passed on information that a plot was being hatched. Later, when Wright approached the King to claim reward for this service he said that he had provided information "for two years space almost before the said treason burst forth by an obscure letter (72)."

There was more than one thread leading to the Plot. Some time between March and August, 1604, one of Cecil's informers named Gage was working hard on Francis Tresham – the Catholic "not known to be of so good example as the rest," whose sister was married to Lord Monteagle. Gage was encouraging Tresham to pass on any information that he might have about "Catholic Plots."

Lord Monteagle's part

Lord Monteagle's role will be looked at more closely later on in the book, but Cecil made quite sure that no one would ever know exactly what part the noble lord played in this twisted tale. When the conspirators were examined, at least some of the things that they said about Monteagle were put down on paper – but these references were later erased or pasted over. Before the plotters were put on trial Cecil wrote confidentially to the Attorney General in his own hand. He warned that the prosecution should tread warily in using Monteagle's name, not only because the King praised him, but also "because it is so lewdly given out that he was once of this powder plot, and afterwards betrayed it all to me (73)."

Now it will be understood why, if the conspirators did dig a tunnel, they managed to avoid detection. This is only guesswork but, supposing that some sharp-eyed or sharp-eared citizen had reported strange happenings around Master Whynniard's house, Robert Cecil would undoubtedly have found a way to silence the informer. Right from the start he knew that a plot was being concocted. There was no need to nip it in the bud.

He wanted it to develop as much as possible, and to involve as many Catholics as Catesby could enlist, before he made all his arrests.

Guy Fawkes's first interrogation after his capture

4 The Monteagle Letter

"The little comedy at Hoxton"

WE COME now to what a modern historian has called "the little comedy at Hoxton." This is the official explanation of how the Gunpowder Plot was discovered.

On the evening of Saturday, 26th October, 1605, Lord Monteagle was at his house at Hoxton, which was then a village outside London. "At seven o'clock of the night one of his footmen, whom he had sent on an errand over the street, was met by an unknown man of reasonable tall personage, who delivered him a letter charging him to put it in my Lord his master's hands. Which my Lord no sooner received but that having broken it up, and perceiving the same to be of unknown and somewhat unlegible hand and without either date or subscription, did call one of his men unto him for helping him to read it.

"But no sooner did he perceive the strange contents thereof, although he was somewhat perplexed . . . yet . . . notwithstanding the lateness and darkness of the night in that season of the year, he presently repaired to his Majesty's palace at Whitehall, and there delivered the same to the Earl of Salisbury (74)."

The "strange contents" that had perplexed Monteagle were as follows: "My lord. Out of the love I bear to some of your friends I have a care of your preservation. Therefore I would advise you, as you tender your life, to devise some excuse to shift of your attendance at this Parliament, for God and man hath concurred to punish the wickedness of this time. And think not slightly of this advertisement but retire yourself into your country, where you may expect the event in safety.

"For though there be no appearance of any stir, yet I say they shall receive a terrible blow this Parliament, and yet they shall not see who hurts them. This counsel is not to be condemned, because it may do you good and can do you no harm, for the danger is passed as soon as you have burned the letter. And I hope God will give you the grace to make good use of it, to whose holy protection I commend you (75)."

Robert Cecil read this cryptic message, and having digested it, said that it reminded him of information "he had received from beyond the seas . . ." He said it was to do with "some business the Papists were in, both at home and abroad, making preparations for some combination amongst them for enabling them to deliver at that time to the King some petition for toleration of religions. It was to be so well backed as the King should be loth to refuse their requests, like the sturdy beggars craving alms with one hand, but carrying a stone in the other, in case of refusal (76)."

James reads the letter

Other members of the Privy Council examined this mysterious letter. They agreed that as soon as King James returned from his hunting trip to Royston it should be shown to him. His Majesty had a "fortunate judgement in clearing and solving of obscure riddles and doubtful mysteries (77)." When James saw the letter he turned it over for some time. He "did thereupon conjecture, that the danger mentioned should be some sudden danger by blowing up of powder. For no other . . . desperate attempt could be committed or attempted in time of Parliament . . . except only if it were by blowing up of powder, which might be performed by one base knave in a dark corner (78)."

It has been pointed out that James, with his stiletto-proof quilted doublets, was a mortal coward. Perhaps he had a complex about "gunpowder plots" generally, because his father, the Earl of Darnley, had been blown up when he lay ill in a desolate house called Kirk o'Fields. Accordingly, it is likely that he would have been alert to hints about powder in the letter received by Monteagle, and that his wrath against the conspirators would be the more terrible because they planned to kill him in the same way that his father had been killed.

In the official account of the Plot's discovery James is cast in

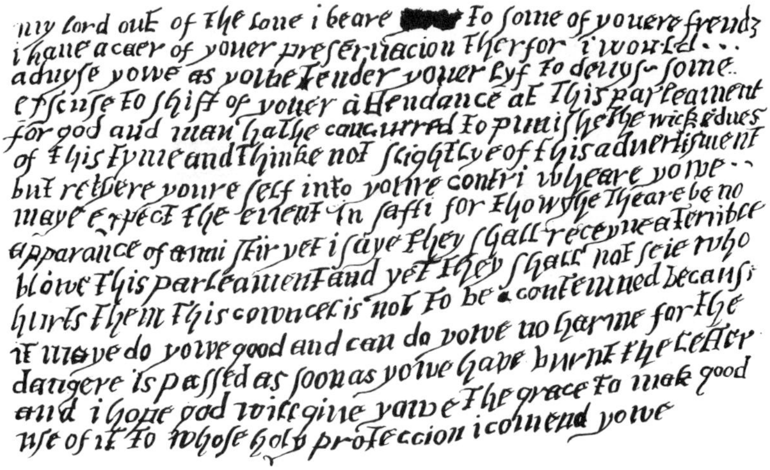
my lord out of the love i beare [redacted] to some of youere frends
i have a caer of youer preservacion therfor i would
advyse yowe as yowe tender youer lyf to devyse some
excuse to shift of youer attendance at this parleament
for god and man hathe concurred to punishe the wickednes
of this tyme and thinke not slightlye of this advertisment
but retyere youre self into youre contri wheare yowe
maye expect the event in saftli for thowghe theare be no
apparance of anni stir yet i saye they shall receyve a terrible
blowe this parleament and yet they shall not seie who
hurts them this cowncel is not to be contemned because
it maye do yowe good and can do yowe no harme for the
dangere is passed as soon as yowe have burnt the letter
and i hope god will give yowe the grace to mak good
use of it to whose holy proteccion i comend yowe

A facsimile of the warning letter sent to Lord Monteagle

the role of the intelligent decipherer of Monteagle's letter. This was sheer flattery, to impress the public with their monarch's wisdom. James knew all about the Plot long before he saw the letter. On 24th October, two days before Monteagle received the letter, and while James was still hunting in Cambridgeshire, Cecil wrote to his friend Sir Thomas Lake: "Let his Majesty know that I dare boldly to say no shower nor storm shall mar our harvest, except it should come from the middle region (79)."

James's knowledge of the Plot

In other words, the London-based conspirators would be "harvested" or gathered in, when it suited Cecil, and according to plan. Those who were scattered through "the middle region" – the Midlands – might still manage to launch their rebellion.

Searching for gunpowder

Once James had seen the threat of explosion – possibly enjoying this impressive bit of play acting – the next step was to find the diabolical powder: "It was determined that the said Lord Chamberlain should, according to his custom and office, view all the Parliament houses both above and below, and consider what likelihood or appearance of danger might be gathered by the sight of them (80)."

This the Lord Chamberlain did, accompanied by an armed

A contemporary Dutch print, showing how the conspirators planned to blow up the Lord's Chamber

escort and Lord Monteagle who was "earnest and curious to see the event of that accident whereof he had the fortune to be the first discoverer . . . He [the Lord Chamberlain] found, in the vault, under the upper house, great store and provision of billets, faggots, and coals."

He asked Whynniard, Keeper of the Wardrobe, to what use he had put those lower rooms and cellars. Whynniard told him that "Thomas Percy had hired both the house, and part of the cellar or vault under the same, and that the wood and coal therein were the said gentleman's own provision . . ."

"The Lord Chamberlain, casting his eye aside, perceived a fellow standing in a corner there, calling himself the said Percy's man, and keeper of that house for him, but indeed was Guido Fawkes (81)."

The Lord Chamberlain looked around "with a heedful indeed, yet, in outward appearance, with but a careless and rackless eye (82)." He went upon his way, pretending to be satisfied. As soon as he returned to the King and Council, however, it was another matter. Thomas Percy was a Catholic, and there was an "extraordinary great provision of wood and coal in that house where Thomas Percy had so seldom occasion to remain (83)." Also there was the "very tall and desperate fellow" in charge. All this added up to something very suspicious. Obviously, another search was necessary, more intensive than the first tour by the Lord Chamberlain.

The conspirators meanwhile had learned, almost certainly through Guy Fawkes, that the government was on their tail. Thomas Winter recalled that on 27th October, "in came one to my chamber and told me that a letter had been given to my Lord Monteagle to this effect; that he wished his lordship's absence from Parliament because a blow would there be given, which he presently carried to my lord of Salisbury (84)."

This alarming news was at once taken to the originator of the Plot by Thomas Winter: "I told it to Mr. Catesby, assuring him withal that the matter was disclosed, and wishing him in any wise to forsake his country (85)."

Catesby did not panic at the news. Instead, he sent Fawkes to see whether their concealed gunpowder had been found and Fawkes – brave to the point of rashness – accepted the mission, and put his head into what could have been a noose. (He was not to know that Cecil was not yet ready to make his arrests.) Fawkes returned to report that the wood which covered the barrels of gunpowder had not been disturbed; his secret marks were still in their correct places.

Catesby and Winter then considered how their project could have leaked. Their suspicions lighted on Francis Tresham. Tresham had already suggested they should abandon the plan, and Lord Monteagle was his brother-in-law. No one knows the details of the conversation between Catesby, Winter and Tresham. It probably began on a grim note, with Catesby and Winter fingering their daggers. Tresham must have been a good talker: with so much at stake the conspirators would have killed him outright if his defence had not sounded good. Whatever he told them, they accepted, and right to the end they regarded him

as one of themselves.

Tresham's true part in the Gunpowder Plot is unlikely to come to light. If he was a loyal conspirator his behaviour is hard to understand, for when Fawkes was arrested Tresham made no attempt to flee. The government did not include his name among the plotters, and he was not arrested until 12th November.

Father Gerard's comments

The comments of the Jesuit, Father John Gerard, are very useful in trying to unravel these strange circumstances. He said that "the gentlemen themselves did most fear Mr. Francis Tresham to be the man that should send this letter unto Lord Monteagle, which lord had married Mr. Tresham's sister, but that was nothing likely (86)."

Gerard guessed that if Monteagle was not to be trusted then Tresham would not have written to him. If he was to be trusted, a letter was unnecessary: a word spoken in his ear would have been enough. Gerard said Tresham "was very witty [*i.e.* intelligent] and surely the sending of such a letter in such a manner was nothing wittily contrived . . . Neither would Mr. Tresham have ventured his life and estate . . . for his brother-in-law, if he had not thought him worthy of further trust . . . If he did not think the letter would persuade, why should he write it so plainly? (87)"

Gerard had some other shrewd comments about the events which were alleged to have taken place at Hoxton. Lord Monteagle was dining at a property which he had not visited for a year, and yet the strange messenger had known exactly where to find him on that dark November night. As the contents of the letter were "dynamite" it seems strange that the tall messenger passed it to a servant just as Monteagle was going in to dinner. Surely he should have given it to Monteagle when he could study it in private? Why send him a letter at all when the conspirators could have found other ways of keeping him from the opening of Parliament? Finally, there was no need to give him ten clear days notice of the impending peril.

Small wonder that Gerard noted how many intelligent men "do persuade themselves that the matter came out by some other means, and that the letter was but framed and sent of purpose to give show of casual discovery, both to hide the true

Opposite Guy Fawkes setting the gunpowder trail

means, and to make the special preservation of the King and State to be better discerned to come from God himself (88)."

Catesby's varied replies

Monteagle was not the only lord who knew, one way or another, that it might be safer to stay away from the opening of Parliament. In a way, the fault that these warnings leaked was Catesby's. When the question of saving Catholics and pro-Catholic lords was put to him, Catesby's replies varied. Sometimes he protested that the nobility deserved to die, as "atheists, fools and cowards (89)." On another occasion he promised that "such of the nobility as are worth saving shall be preserved, and yet shall not know of the matter (90)." Once, in his fury, the leader of the conspirators cried that, "rather than the project should not take effect, if they were as dear unto me as my own son, they must also be blown up (91)."

Since Catesby failed to provide proper assurance that anyone would be saved, it seems that each conspirator pursued his own policy. Sir Everard Digby admitted that "I had some friends that were in danger, which I prevented (92)." Lords Montague, Mordaunt and Stourton were among the peers who knew that it would be better to stay at home on 5th November.

Lord Monteagle's part

The betrayal of the Gunpowder Plot is a mystery, which historians have failed to solve over the past three hundred and fifty years. One of the likeliest explanations is that Lord Monteagle, with a foot in both the Catholic-conspiratorial camp and the government's, revealed the Plot to Robert Cecil. Cecil with his network of secret-service agents, had already an idea of what was happening. It was undesirable that Monteagle should be seen to the world as a common informer, and so "the little comedy" of the tall man with his unsigned letter was invented.

Meanwhile, Tresham had been lured into the conspirators' ranks, and at some stage had panicked and warned his brother-in-law to avoid the opening of Parliament. Monteagle probably thanked Tresham, and then explained that the Plot was already betrayed.

Tresham tried to save the conspirators' lives as he had Monteagle's, but he was afraid to tell them everything he knew. His only hope was to dissuade them from their plan. When he failed to do this he thought he would be safe in London because he had demonstrated his loyalty to the King by talking to Monteagle. Either he did not expect to be arrested, or he was confident of early release.

The conspirators take their posts

"The suspicion of all hands put us into such confusion (93)," said Thomas Winter. But on the afternoon of Monday, 4th November it still looked as if the Plot might succeed. Catesby left London for the Midlands; he knew that whether Fawkes managed to blow up Parliament or not, the government was onto the conspirators' scent and would eventually find out who exactly they were; the attempt to seize Princess Elizabeth had to go ahead.

Ambrose Rookwood, with relays of fast horses waiting at strategic points, planned to leave London on the 5th. Hopefully, he would be able to carry the news to Robert Catesby that the King, Robert Cecil and many others had been blown sky-high. Robert Keyes took a watch from Thomas Percy to Guy Fawkes, so that Fawkes might time his actions precisely in setting a slow fuse alight and then making his escape. Having done this Keyes settled down in London with Christopher Wright and Percy. John Wright rode off during the afternoon to catch up with Catesby. Fawkes received the watch from Percy on 4th November at 10 o'clock. Two hours later he was arrested.

Fawkes's arrest

"Sir Thomas Knyvet, a gentleman of his Majesty's Privy Chamber . . . went . . . , about the midnight next after [4th November] to the Parliament house, accompanied with such a small number as was fit for that errand; but before his entry into the house, finding Thomas Percy's alleged man standing without the doors, his clothes and boots on, at so dead a time of the night, he resolved to apprehend him; as he did, and thereafter went forward to the searching of the house, where, after he had caused to be overturned some of the billets and coals, he first found one of the small barrels of powder, and afterwards all the rest to the number of thirty-six barrels great and small; and thereafter searching the fellow whom he had taken, found three matches, and all other instruments fit for blowing up the powder, ready upon him (94)."

Fawkes defiant

Guy Fawkes, if the official story is true, was defiant, telling

Knyvet, "that if he had happened to be within the house, when he took him, as he was immediately before [at the ending of his work] he would not have failed to blow him up, house and all (95)."

In the circumstances, it did not seem unreasonable to wake the King, although it was just 4 o'clock in the morning. As for Fawkes, "all that day the Council could get nothing out of him, touching his accomplices, refusing to answer any such questions which he thought might discover the plot (96)."

It may be true that Fawkes revealed nothing at that stage, and indeed the government said that it was only on 9th November that he cracked under torture, but it is significant that on the 5th the government had seized servants of the plotters and others connected with them and begun interrogation. This is clear proof that many details of the plot and the plotters were known before the 5th. What is surprising is the fact that all the conspirators were able to escape from London.

At about 5 o'clock on the morning of the 5th November a haggard Christopher Wright appeared at Thomas Winter's lodgings at "The Duck and Drake." He told Winter there was much to-ing and fro-ing in the Strand and "withal, the matter is discovered (97)." From these words that Wright reported it was clear to Winter that the hue-and-cry was raised for Thomas Percy.

"A treason discovered"

Winter later confessed how he immediately instructed Wright: "Go you then to Mr. Percy, for sure it is for him they seek, and bid him be gone. I will stay and see the uttermost." He then went on: "Then I went to the Court gates and found them straitly guarded, so as nobody could enter. From thence I went down towards the Parliament house, and in the middle of King Street found the Guard standing that would not let me pass. And as I returned I heard one say, 'There is a treason discovered in which the King and the lords should have been blown up.' So then I was fully satisfied that all was known and went to the stable where my gelding stood, and rode into the country (98)."

Rookwood had already left London with the bad news. He made fast time, at one stage covering thirty miles in two hours on one horse. First he overtook Keyes, next Percy and

Opposite Christopher Wright, another conspirator in the Plot

Christopher Wright, and last of all Catesby and John Wright. Before long, "notwithstanding the foulness of the winter ways," the six conspirators rode into Catesby's house at Ashby St. Legers at about 6 o'clock, just as Lady Catesby and Thomas Winter's brother, who had come over from Huddington, were sitting down to dinner.

Their news was scarcely likely to improve anyone's appetite, but Catesby was too good a leader to shatter his friend's morale with a dramatic public announcement that the Plot had totally collapsed. On the other hand, he could not bring himself to deceive Robert, the brother of his close friend Thomas Winter. Robert Winter later explained: "Catesby sent for me into the fields . . . and willed me to take my horse and come and speak to him . . . So I went to him, who told me that Mr. Fawkes was taken and the whole Plot discovered (99)."

Although this is what Robert Winter may have told his interrogators, or it is what they chose to write down, it cannot be exactly what Catesby said. "The whole Plot" included a revolt in the Midlands, and although Robert Cecil's agents knew something about this, there is no reason to suppose that Catesby was aware of that fact. Even if Cecil knew of the Plot, it did not mean that it was doomed to failure. In fact, it was to this part of the total programme that Catesby now devoted his energies.

After their visit to Ashby St. Legers the conspirators set out towards Dunchurch, where Sir Everard Digby had organized a hunting match. There, it was believed, the Catholic gentlemen who had so cheerfully accepted an invitation to sport would just as cheerfully draw their swords in rebellion.

Catesby, at this point, was up to his old game of telling the others what he considered it best for them to hear, with no strict regard for the truth. He took Digby aside and explained that although the London end of the Plot had not gone quite according to plan, both King James and Robert Cecil were dead. Digby said he had learned from Catesby that, "there was such a pudder [confusion] bred in the state . . . as if true Catholics would now stir he doubted not but that they might procure to themselves good conditions (100)."

The arrest of Guy Fawkes

Guy Fawkes was interrogated many times.

Having told an outright lie, Catesby continued to outline a wild scheme which could not be expected to materialize. He said that the Littletons, a Catholic family, would bring in 1,000 armed men, and Robert Winter's father-in-law was good for even more. The army would march through Warwickshire and Worcestershire, picking up men as it went, and this western rising would trigger off Catholic action elsewhere in the country.

Catesby's strategy

It soon became clear that this sort of optimism was totally unfounded. The guests at the Dunchurch hunt recoiled in horror when they found out why they had been assembled, and left as fast as their horses would carry them. Sir Everard's own uncle, Sir Robert Digby, called the conspirators traitors to their faces, and thundered away.

No Catholic support

When the conspirators left Dunchurch it was not with an enthusiastic little army of gentlemen and their servants. Catesby headed only fifty men, and not all of these had their hearts in the work. One of Digby's servants protested that he was not "privy to this bloody faction," and yet because he was in Digby's service he would be presumed guilty. "What was to become of him, and the rest of his poor servants?" Digby's answer was scarcely comforting: "Now there is no remedy (101)."

When morale is low, bickering often follows. On nearing Warwick, Catesby suggested that they should go into the town and raid the stables of a horse breaker as this would at least give them a chance to change their jaded mounts for fresh ones. Robert Winter objected. He calculated that while local people might not involve themselves in politics they would certainly turn out in pursuit of a band of horse thieves.

Arguments of that nature cut little ice with Catesby, who better than any of them recognized the desperate nature of the game they were playing. "Some of us may not look back," he said.

Either Robert Winter was a simpler soul, or he could not face up to the appalling prospect that confronted them all as unsuccessful rebels, because he replied: "But others, I hope may, and therefore I pray you let this alone."

"What, hast thou any hope, Robin?" asked Catesby incredulously. "I assure thee there is none that knoweth of this action but shall perish (102)."

Desperate circumstances demand desperate action, and so despite Winter's objection the conspirators stole nine or ten horses at Warwick.

During the ride westward the conspirators became even more depressed. John Grant joined the band with arms and armour that he had brought from London, but there were scarcely enough men to use them. Father Garnet sent a message that could have given them little encouragement: "I marvelled that they would enter into such wicked activities and not be ruled by the advice of their friends and the orders of his Holiness (103)." And Father Tesimond thought that "all Catholics were undone (104)" because of the conspiracy.

Attempts to raise a rebellion

As they moved towards Holbeach, where the mansion of the friendly Littleton family was situated, four men rode at the head of the cavalcade and four behind. They did this "to keep the company from starting away," but odd conscripts still managed to straggle off into the gloom.

What happened at Hewell Grange could be typical of many disappointments that they suffered. Catesby rode up to some twenty or thirty villagers, who watched the arrival of the armed men and their carts with curiosity, and asked them if they would join him.

"It may be, if we know what you mean to do," said one countryman, demonstrating a proper combination of enterprise and caution.

"We are for God and the country," replied Catesby. It was the sort of meaningless, or diplomatic, reply that we have heard him give on other tricky occasions. However, the villagers' spokesman turned out to be the conspirator's match for he struck his stick on the ground, as if to give his words emphasis, and his reply suggests that those countryfolk had got a hint of what was in the wind: "We are for the King James, as well as for God and the country, and we will not go against his will (105)."

The total failure of the efforts to recruit were summed up by Sir Everard Digby: "Not one man came to take our part, though we expected so many (106)."

The Sheriff's posse

By the time Catesby and his men reached Holbeach House at 10 o'clock their plight was desperate. They had lost some of their original band and had gathered no new help. Worst of all, they were being pursued. In the gathering gloom they had seen riders whom they first thought were friendly Catholics, but who turned out to be the Worcestershire posse led by the Sheriff, Sir Richard Walsh. Though small, the posse was relentless. It would stick to the trail until reinforcements arrived and the conspirators could be attacked.

Gunpowder explosion

Next morning, Friday, 8th November, Thomas Winter left Holbeach House in a last effort to find support among the local Catholics. In his absence a catastrophe occurred to the men left behind: "Some of them standing by the fire side, and having set two pounds and a half of powder to dry in a platter before the fire, and underset the platter with a great linen bag full of other powder, containing some fifteen or sixteen pounds; it so fell out, that one coming to put more wood into the fire, and casting it on, there flew a coal into the platter, by reason whereof the powder taking fire and blowing up, scorched those who were nearest (107)."

Conspirators flee

Winter heard about the news from his servant: "My man came to me and said a heavy mischance had severed all the company, for that Mr. Catesby, Mr. Rookwood and Mr. Grant were burnt with gunpowder, upon which sight the rest dispersed. Master Littleton wished me to fly, and so would he. I told him, I would first see the body of my friend and bury him, whatsoever befell me (108)."

When Winter returned to Holbeach he found things were bad enough, but not so bad as his servant had suggested. No one was dead, although Grant was "much disfigured and his eyes almost burned out (109)." Littleton, Digby, Robert Winter, and Bates had fled, so the conspirators no longer existed as an organized band. Ironically, it was gunpowder, which was to have been the solution to their problem, that in the end drove the final nail into the coffin of their hopes. Father John Gerard said: "They took it as a sign of God's will that he would not have them prepare to resist, but rather to prepare themselves to suffer . . . They all fell earnestly to their prayers (110)."

Winter then enquired what the next step should be: "I asked them [the remaining conspirators] what they resolved to do.

Overleaf The fight at Holbeach House between the conspirators and the Sheriff's posse (8th November, 1605)

They answered, we mean here to die. I said again, I would take such part as they did (111)."

About noon the Sheriff arrived with his reinforced posse, and delivered an ultimatum. "The greatest part of their retinue and some of the better sort being dispersed and fled before our coming, whereupon and after summons and warning first given in his Highnesses name to yield and submit themselves, who refusing the same, we fired some part of the house, and assaulted some part of the rebellious persons left in the house (112)."

There were several hundred of the Sheriff's attackers, and many of them were armed with muskets. They were opposed by Catesby, Percy, Rookwood, Thomas Winter, the two Wrights, and the half-blind Grant, with six others. Of these six, just one was from the Dunchurch hunting party, from which so much had been expected.

The cowardly Sheriff

The Sheriff seems to have been a man who feared bloodshed for it was complained that he "kept himself close under the wall" so that "he could not see what was done within (113)."

The death of Catesby and Percy

Although the conspirators had "resolved that they would not be taken, but rather suffer death at that time in the field (114)," Thomas Winter's account shows how he at least was thwarted in this intention: "As I walked into the court I was shot in the shoulder which lost me the use of my arm; the next shot was the elder Wright struck dead; after him the younger Mr. Wright; and fourthly Ambrose Rookwood. Then said Mr. Catesby, standing before the door they were to enter, 'Stand by me, Tom, and we will die together.' 'Sir,' quoth I, 'I have lost the use of my right arm, and I fear that will cause me to be taken.' So as we stood close together, Mr. Catesby, Mr. Percy and myself, they two were shot, as far as I could guess, with one bullet, and then the company entered upon me, hurt me in the belly with a pike, and gave me other wounds (115)."

The skirmish had not shown the attackers, who relied upon their muskets rather than their swords, to any great advantage, and what followed was equally unheroic. The one Staffordshire man present, Sir Thomas Lawley, tried to "revive Catesby, Percy and the two Wrights, who lay deadly wounded upon the ground, thinking by the recovery of them to have done unto his Majesty better service than by suffering them to die . . ." He goes on: "But such was the extreme disorder of the baser sort, that while I with my men took up one of the languishing traitors, the rude people stripped the rest naked, their wounds being many and grievous and no surgeon at hand, they became incurable and so died (116)."

Sir Thomas's letter to Robert Cecil shows it was not only "the baser sort" who laid hands on whatever they could: "In the hurly burly my man that took Thomas Winter seized his horse, which I keep to the King's use. Now the Sheriff of Staffordshire who was not at that service, nor any gentleman of Staffordshire but myself, demands of me the horse, which I refuse to deliver unto him until I know your further pleasure therein (117)."

There might have been some petty bickering about a horse, but the Gunpowder Plot was over, except for the shouting. Some of the conspirators were dead, notably Robert Catesby and Thomas Percy. Thomas Winter, John Grant and Ambrose Rookwood were patched up and sent to the Tower of London, where Robert Keyes, Sir Everard Digby and Thomas Bates – who were soon captured – joined them. Francis Tresham was arrested on 12th November, which meant that only Robert Winter of the original plotters was at large, along with the Littletons.

Procerum
Primogeniti

5 Trial and Execution

King James's speech

THE FIGHT between the conspirators and the Sheriff's posse at Holbeach House took place on 8th November, 1605. On Saturday, 9th November, King James gave Parliament his account of "this great and horrible attempt, whereof the like was never either heard or read." The story of what the conspirators had intended improved in the telling. King James recounted that not only had they planned "the destruction of my person, nor of my wife and posterity only, but of the whole body of the state in general . . . The whole nobility, the whole reverend clergy, bishops and most part of the good preachers, the most part of the gentry . . . the whole judges of the land, with most of the lawyers and the whole clerks (118)."

The aim of this speech was to make as many people as possible feel that they had been threatened by this Catholic plot. When the text of James's speech was published all Catholics found themselves tarred with the same brush as the handful of conspirators. The King said: "None of those that truly know and believe the whole . . . grounds of their doctrine can ever prove either good Christians or faithful subjects (119)."

A Thanksgiving day

But the citizens of London had not been required to await publication of the royal speech in order to learn about the Plot. Sunday, 10th November, had been declared a day of thanksgiving in all churches, and every clergyman preached his own loyal sermon. William Barlow, Bishop of Rochester, who was chosen to preach the official sermon at St. Paul's Cross said the Plot was "a cruel execution, an inhuman cruelty, a brutal inhumanity, a devilish brutishness, an hyperbolical, yea, an hyperbolical

Opposite James I in Parliament

devilishness (120)."

With the authority of the King and clergy behind them, the pamphlet writers could safely join in the anti-Catholic campaign. The Catholic Archpriest, George Blackwell, tried to make amends by issuing a letter to all Catholics, condemning "the unlawfulness of the late desparate attempt against our gracious sovereign (121)," but it was in vain. The government was determined to discredit and incriminate as many Catholics as possible – the Pope, the exiles in Flanders, the Catholic nobles, and most specially the much-hated Jesuits. If the evidence was not immediately available for such a policy then it could be extracted; if it could not be extracted then it would be fabricated. The starting point for this course of action was the interrogation of the captured conspirators.

Guy Fawkes was the first plotter to fall into government hands and the King had seen him within a few hours of capture. But, despite Robert Cecil's observation that the King had "fortunate judgement in clearing and solving of obscure riddles and doubtful mysteries," James was still mystified by the Yorkshireman. He commented: "I can never yet hear of any man that knows him (122)." So he drew up a list of questions that had to be answered by Fawkes. Some of them are what might be expected, but others cast light on James's naturally inquisitive nature. Why, for example, did he want to know how Fawkes "received these wounds in his breast?" or "when and where he learned to speak French?"

Fawkes unruffled

According to Cecil, when Fawkes was seized he showed himself "no more dismayed – nay, scarcely more troubled than if he was taken for some poor robbery on the highway (123)." Forty-eight hours later Fawkes was still unruffled. Sir William Waad, Lieutenant of the Tower of London, and himself a great worrier, marvelled that Fawkes had "taken such rest this night as a man void of all trouble of mind (124)." This Fawkes was able to do even though he knew what lay in store for him. He told Waad that although he had taken an oath of secrecy, he "knew not what torture might do (125)." Waad had arranged and supervised the torture of a good many men during his career, and he promised Cecil results in the case of Fawkes: "I

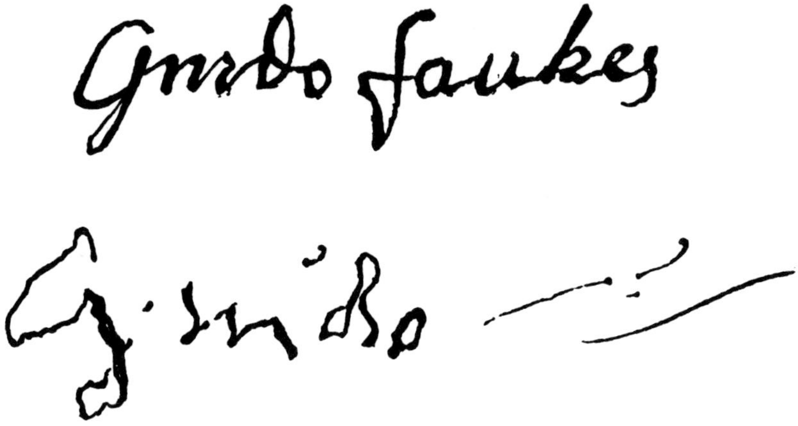

The autographs of Guy Fawkes before and after torture

am confident, notwithstanding his resolute mind, in the end he will be more open (126)."

The King gave precise order how Fawkes was to be tortured: "The gentler tortures are to be first used unto him, *et sic per gradus ad ima tenditur* [and so on to the very worst]." He ended this order with unspeakable hypocrisy: "And so God speed your good work (127)."

Fawkes confesses

Fawkes was resolute, showing "a most stubborn and perverse humour, as dogged as if he were possessed (128)." He led Waad to suppose that he would tell all and then revealed nothing, which may have been a brave attempt to give the other plotters time to get away. The first time that he was put on the rack he stayed silent, but the warning that "he must come to it again and again, from day to day, till he should have delivered his whole knowledge (129)," must have daunted him. He was tortured repeatedly, and his last piece of evidence was not signed until 17th November. By then he was a broken man. His final signature is one scrawled word – "Guido" – followed by two faint marks as if he had collapsed before he could summon the strength to complete his surname.

Guy Fawkes was not one of the originators of the Plot, and although he could tell his persecutors how it developed he could cast no new light on the intentions of the dead Catesby. Even more regrettable from Cecil's point of view was his failure to incriminate the exiles in Flanders, the English nobility, or the Jesuits. Cecil looked at the confessions as they had been taken down verbatim, and added a stroke or two of his quill. It is still possible to see the improvements he made on the original documents. By the time the confession was printed it excluded a statement that Fawkes made absolving the Jesuits from complicity in the Plot, and it included a statement that he never made, which named some of the Flanders exiles as accomplices.

Fawkes was the only prisoner to be officially tortured, although the others may have suffered in the same way. A note from Cecil can certainly be interpreted as indicating that several were put on the rack: "Most of the conspirators here wilfully forswear that the priests knew anything in particular, and obstinately refuse to be accusers of them, yea, what tortures soever they be put to (130)."

One man whose evidence never saw the light of day was Francis Tresham. He was arrested on 12th November and lodged in the Tower, where he suddenly fell ill. Thereafter, all is a mystery. On 15th December he wrote a long letter to Robert Cecil, the contents of which are unknown because it has never been found. On 16th December Tresham was seen by three doctors who came to inspect his health, but their report is also lost. "Butler, the great physician of Cambridge (131)," examined him by placing a piece of "pure gold" in his mouth, and then announced that he had been poisoned. This seems an unusual way of making a diagnosis and was probably mere mumbo-jumbo to impress the audience. If Butler had been a good doctor he would surely have detected other symptoms of poisoning.

Death of Francis Tresham

On 23rd December, Sir William Waad reported Tresham's death to Cecil: "He died this night, about two o'clock after midnight, with very much pain . . . It will not be possible to keep him, for he smelled exceedingly when I was with him yesterday afternoon (132)." And so the remains of Francis Tresham were first beheaded and then "tumbled into a hole . . . without so much ceremony as the formality of a grave (133)." This indecent haste to get him under ground suggests that a post-mortem, even of the crude type that the seventeenth-century offered, would have provided awkward information on the exact way that he died.

If Tresham had lived he would have been a danger to both Lord Monteagle and Robert Cecil as he could have told the world how he had been induced to join the conspiracy and then repented; how he had approached his brother-in-law, Monteagle, and suggested that they should inform the authorities of what was afoot; and how Monteagle had replied that it was best to let things take their course.

It is also probable that Monteagle had disclosed to him that Robert Cecil knew of the Plot, and was just waiting to swoop on the conspirators in his own good time. If this is what happened Tresham would have quickly realized that Monteagle, the supposed friend of the conspirators and also a favourite of the King, was the man who had betrayed the Plot. Such knowledge made him a very marked man. He could have ruined Monteagle's reputation and could also talk about Cecil's devious ways of working. It is therefore almost certain that one – or both – of these men arranged his murder.

Bates incriminates the Jesuits

The most important confession that the government obtained was that of Thomas Bates. His was the sole confession that incriminated the Jesuits. Either under threats, or freely, Bates claimed that he had confessed the Plot to Father Oswald Tesimond, who "bade him obey his master, because it was for a good cause, and be secret, and mention the matter to no other priest (134)."

However, the Jesuit version of what happened is quite contradictory to the government's claim: "This fellow [Bates] being earnestly urged by persons of great authority to confess some proofs or likelihood that the Jesuits were in this action, the poor man, of frailty and desire of life, as afterwards himself affirmed, told them that his master and another of those gentlemen had not been past a fortnight before the action broke out, at a nobleman's house where three Jesuits were, to wit, Father Henry Garnet, Father Oswald Tesimond, and Father John Gerard . . . He thought Father Tesimond did know of the Plot,

Overleaf Westminster Hall where Guy Fawkes, Thomas and Robert Winter, John Grant, Robert Keyes, Thomas Bates, Ambrose Rookwood and Sir Everard Digby were tried

Thomas Bates, the only conspirator whose confession incriminated the Jesuits

which yet he affirmed not of the other two . . . This was no proof at all, but only the single conceit of one simple man, and that only set down as a mere thought of his own head (135)."

It scarcely matters what poor Bates said. His statement is one more document that vanished early on. A copy, or more likely an edited version, was filed for official use. Torture had failed to build a case against the Jesuits, so Bates's words would suffice as "the ground and the only foundation upon which they built that great and slanderous calumnation against all the Jesuits in England (136)."

The trial

On 27th January, 1606, the eight surviving conspirators were brought to trial in Westminster Hall. They were Guy Fawkes, Thomas and Robert Winter, John Grant, Robert Keyes, Thomas Bates, Ambrose Rookwood, and Sir Everard Digby. Nevertheless, the first names that were read out in the indictment were not those of the men at the bar nor those of the men who died at Holbeach. Father Garnet, Father Tesimond and Father Gerard, none of whom had been captured, let alone questioned, were the ones described as the originators of the Plot.

A seventeenth-century trial was not held to determine a man's guilt. The first examinations were the real trial, and the evidence that was obtained during these examinations was produced at the trial to prove the prisoner's guilt. Everyone knew this, including the prisoners themselves. Accused men were not allowed a defence counsel, so that unless they were quick witted – and confinement and ill-treatment were not ideal conditions for keeping a man's wits sharp – they were unable to offer much opposition to the carefully prepared speech of a professional advocate.

Sir Edward Coke's prosecution

The Gunpowder Plotters were prosecuted by the Attorney General, Sir Edward Coke. He was a learned, brilliant and cunning bully. He lived in an age when fluent but brief language was not considered a virtue, and his promise to be "somewhat more copious and not so succinct as my usual manner hath been (137)," must have delighted those who enjoyed a good long speech. The opportunity to speak of what he called "the greatest treasons that ever were plotted in England and concern the greatest king that ever was of England (138)" saw Coke at his

Overleaf The prisoners spent several days in the Tower of London before being executed

best. His speech was studded with a vast collection of quotations from the Bible and from Latin authors, historical allusions, puns and bad jokes.

Every so often, for good measure, Coke would throw in what can only be described as purple passages: "Miserable desolation! No king, no queen, no issue male, no councillors of state, no nobility, no bishops, no judges! Oh, barbarous and more than Scythian or Thracian cruelty! No mantle of holiness can cover it, no pretence of religion can excuse it, no shadow of good intentions can extenuate it. God and Heaven condemn it, man and earth detest it, the offenders themselves were ashamed of it, wicked people exclaim against it, and the souls of all true Christian subjects abhor it (139)."

A traitor's end

It probably did not bother Coke that he too was guilty of "more than Scythian or Thracian cruelty" when he reminded the prisoners in every gory detail of the way in which a convicted traitor met his end: "To be drawn to the place of his execution from his prison, as being not worthy any more to tread upon the face of the earth . . . Also, for that he hath been retrograde to nature, therefore is he drawn backward at a horse's tail. And whereas God made the head of man the highest and most supreme part . . . he must be drawn with his head declining downwards, and lying so near the ground as may be, being thought unfit to take benefit of common air. For which cause also shall he be strangled, being hanged up by the neck between heaven and earth, as deemed unworthy of both or either. . .

He goes on: "Then is he to be cut down alive and to have his privy parts cut off and burned before his face as being unworthily begotten and unfit to leave any generation after him. His bowels and inlaid parts taken out and burned, who inwardly hath conceived and harboured in his heart such horrible treason. After, to have his head cut off, which had imagined the mischief. And lastly his body to be quartered (140)."

After Coke's speech the jury retired and in due course returned to deliver the inevitable verdict of guilty. The eight prisoners were led back from Westminster Hall to the Tower, where they spent their two or three days before execution. Their last hours were not eased by the visits of friends, relatives or priests, all of whom were forbidden to attend. They spent most of their time in prayer, although Sir Everard Digby found sufficient composure of mind to write some verses (141):

Who's that which knocks? oh stay, my Lord, I come:
I know that call, since first it made me know
My self, which makes me now with joy to run,
Lest He be gone that can my duty show.
Jesu, my Lord, I know Thee by the Cross
Thou offer'st me, but not unto my loss.

Come in, my Lord, Whose presence most I crave,
And show Thy will unto my longing mind;
From punishments of sin Thy servant save,
Though he hath been to Thy deserts unkind.
Jesu forgive, and strengthen so my mind,
That rooted virtues thou in me maist find.

Stay still, my Lord, else they fade away,
As Marigold that mourns for absent Sun:
Thou know'st Thou plantest in a barren clay
That chokes in Winter all that up is come;
I do not fear thy Summers wished for heat
My tears shall water where thy shine doth threat.

The Gunpowder Plot is such a sordid story that it comes as a relief to find occasional incidents of nobility. When most people were making intense efforts to prove their total loyalty to the government and no criticism of any aspect of its conduct was likely, Sir Arthur Gorges wrote a spirited but polite letter to Robert Cecil: "Hearing that this present afternoon there was a scaffold setting up very near and right against the fairest gate of Paul's Church, whereupon to torture and quarter these wicked and bloody conspirators, in my poor judgement I did not think it a fit place to be defiled with the blood of such wretches, nor to make a butchery in the churchyard, and under the eaves of the most famous church in our kingdom. . .

"Lastly, I well remember that that was the place of happy memory . . . where our late dread and dear sovereign Elizabeth offered up in all humility upon her knees her thanksgiving to God for the great victory upon the Spaniards, and therefore too

Overleaf The execution of the Gunpowder conspirators

Guy Fawkes just before his execution

worthy to be now polluted with gibbets, hangmen, or the blood of traitors (142)."

Execution of conspirators

Cecil, however, thought otherwise. He was well pleased to associate the defeat of the Armada, which was a great triumph for Protestant England, with the death of the wretched plotters, which could be claimed as an equally great triumph. On 30th January, 1606, Sir Everard Digby, Robert Winter, John Grant and Thomas Bates were drawn upon hurdles to their place of execution at St. Paul's. The following day it was the turn of Thomas Winter, Ambrose Rookwood, Robert Keyes and Guy Fawkes.

Ambrose Rookwood's farewell

Rookwood asked that when his hurdle came to the place where his wife was watching he should be told. He then "opened his eyes (which before he had kept shut to attend better to his prayers) and seeing her stand in a window to see him pass by, he raised himself as well as he could up from the hurdle and said aloud unto her, 'Pray for me, pray for me.' She answered him also aloud. 'I will, and be of good courage and offer thyself wholly to God. I for my part do as freely restore thee to God as He gave thee unto me' (143)."

Last words

In the seventeenth century condemned men were usually expected to make some sort of dying speech upon the scaffold, and most of the conspirators said a few words. Neither Thomas Winter nor Rookwood can be said to have played to the gallery. Winter reminded the crowd that none of the Jesuits had any part in the Plot. Rookwood was more outrageous; he "prayed God to make the King a Catholic (144)."

The last conspirator to die was Guy Fawkes: "His body being weak with torture and sickness, he was scarce able to go up the ladder, but yet with much ado, by the help of the hangman, went high enough to break his neck with the fall (145)."

Gun Powder Treason.

6 Fear and Flight

Claiming rewards

BECAUSE THE GUNPOWDER PLOT is a story of almost unrelieved tragedy there can be no harm in looking first at one of the less grim results. This was the desire of anyone even remotely associated with the Plot's detection or suppression to cash in on their good fortune. Robert Cecil's office was flooded with letters and petitions from such optimists.

John Streete, who claimed to have killed Thomas Percy, Robert Catesby and John Wright, and to have wounded Ambrose Rookwood, pleaded that – after his display of lethal markmanship – he "spared no cost to provide chirurgery [medical treatment] and all other means for the preservation of their lives that were sore hurt, attending them hither at his own charges." As the King had promised £1,000 for Percy alive, plus his whole estate, Streete prayed "for the said £1,000, or a pension (146)."

Secret symbols

Sir William Waad, besides having responsibility for guarding the prisoners, exercised his ingenious mind in other directions. He advised Cecil "to send to the commissioners for a fair scarf that Rookwood made . . . By the figures or ciphers something may be gathered, and if that scarf which Percy had could be discovered it were well it were seen. I perceive there were very many fair scarves made for divers of them, and it were not amiss to learn of the embroiderers what scarves of such sort have lately been made and for whom (147)." Presumably he hoped that the conspirators and their supporters had all adopted some secret emblem, and once this was detected a mass roundup of Catholic militants would be possible.

Opposite A contemporary pamphlet shows the eye of God watching the conspirators

The lantern that Guy Fawkes used in the room below the Lords' Chamber

est et cum qua deprehensus
rranea vbi domo Parlamenti
Ex dono Rob: Heywood nuper
ratoris, Apr. 4o. 1641,

Precautions and celebrations

Even officials who were not remotely connected with the Plot used its discovery as an opportunity to show their loyalty. Alban Stepneth, Sheriff of distant Pembrokeshire, was one of these: "I have caused due watch to be set along all the sea coasts in this county, that no strangers or suspected persons shall take shipping or pass beyond the seas before they be examined. In joy and thanksgiving for the preservation of the King we have caused bonfires to be made, and the bells to be rung, and prayers to be celebrated accordingly. This poor and little county of Pembrokeshire is free from all treason and treacherous practices, and filled with the most faithful subjects (148)."

Informers

With the country on the brink of spy mania, and Cecil known to be the employer and manipulator of agents, all sorts of people offered their services. Benjamin Hewes reported that Sir William Cob of Norfolk was back from the Continent "and likely by the company he was conversant with to be one of the horrible conspirators . . . If Salisbury pleases to employ him he hopes to find Cob (149)."

Another would-be informer was Richard Jones: "Sir Francis Smythe rode out of London the Monday before this most traitorous conspiracy should have been put into execution, and returned not until Tuesday week after, when it should seem he had ridden very hard, for the Wednesday following his horse was so weary that he could not rise when Jones kicked him as he lay in the stable at the Red Lion in Holborn (150)."

Suggested punishments

A certain Thomas Elliot, "as dangerous and enterprising a fellow as can be," stooped so low as to inform Lord Salisbury's servant Richard Percival of "diverse wild words . . . against the King" by Margaret Trem, who with her husband he judged to be "the worst recusants in Dorsetshire." Doubtless, Elliot knew this was rather lightweight stuff for a good intelligence agent, so for extra weight he threw in a petition expressing his joy at the King's escape from "devilish, arrogant, perverse and damned traitors, seminary priests, Jesuits and Papists." These people, he suggested, should be "lapped up alive in lead with their arms spread abroad, and set upon the highest pinnacle in every city and port town in England, and let them there starve to death." It also seemed a good idea that "near every church should be

Robert Cecil, Earl of Salisbury

built a pair of gallows or gibbets, and all Papists and wilful recusants hanged there (151)."

Almost as unpleasant as Elliot was Susan, Countess of Kent. "She has knowledge that Mr. William Willughby [sic] should be one of this most hateful treason. His living in Suffolk is but £200, which by his most foul act is rightly his Majesty's. She asks if Salisbury is willing she should beg it of his Majesty; or if Willughby be free, some other of the like estate of living to help her extreme hard estate (152)."

Cecil was not famous for his sense of humour, and it is difficult to imagine his reaction when the loyal, but atrocious puns, of John Favor, vicar of Halifax, were forwarded to his notice: "Percy, Pierce-eye. Percy would pierce the eye of king and state (153)."

Anonymous letters

Finally, there were letters from cranks: "You are admonished that there are five who have undertaken your death . . . if you continue plotting these stratagems against recusants. None of the five know who the other four be. It is agreed who shall first attempt it by shot, and who shall follow. Death will willingly be embraced for preventing the calamities which you threaten to us all. We protest that we know no other means left us, since you seem but as a match to give fire to his Majesty (154)."

Among the conspirators who fled from Holbeach House on Friday, 8th November, after the accidental explosion, there were Thomas Winter's brother, Robert, and Stephen Littleton. They took refuge in Hagley House, Worcestershire, the home of Stephen's cousin, "Red Humphrey" Littleton. Red Humphrey was a gossip, and word soon escaped where these men were hiding. It was not long before they were captured and condemned to death.

Littleton's treachery

Once again Humphrey's tongue wagged, but now he was a captive and bargaining for his life. Sir Richard Lewkenor who had charge of Humphrey Littleton said: "Humphrey Littleton offered to do good service if his execution might be respited but until your Lordships might be advertised of such discoveries as he could make of certain Jesuits and priests, which had been persuaders of him and others to these actions (155)."

Littleton believed that the Jesuit, Father Oldcorne, and possibly others, might be concealed in Thomas Abington's house at Hindlip, near Worcester. So, on the morning of Sunday, 19th January, Sir Henry Bromley arrived at Hindlip with a posse of over one hundred men to see if this belief was true: "Beginning to beat at the gate with great importunity to be let in presently, the Catholics within the house, soon perceiving their intention, made all possible haste to hide both the priests and the Church stuff . . . The knight being entered by force . . . began after the accustomed manner to go through all the rooms of the house, which were many and very large . . . They searched and sounded [but] . . . found no likelihood of finding what they came for, though they continued the daily search. . .

Hindlip searched

"But upon Saturday two laymen that did usually attend upon the two priests and were hid in a place apart by themselves, being almost starved to death came out of their own accord . . . They had but one apple between them in all those six or seven days . . . These two virtuous men being in hope that upon their taking the searchers would be satisfied and depart (156)."

One of the two men was Nicholas Owen, the greatest architect of the superbly constructed hidden chambers which are to be found in many houses, and which, from their intended purpose, are called Priests' Holes. Despite their hunger these two made a brave bid for freedom: "Perceiving that some of the searchers did continually by turns watch and walk up and down in the room where they were hidden, which was a long and fair gallery four square, going round the house, they watched their time when the searchers were furthest off, and came out so secretly and stilly, and shut the place again so finely, that they were not one whit heard or perceived when and where they came out, and so they walked in the gallery towards the door which they thought belike to have found open. But the searchers being turned back in their walk, and perceiving two strange men to be there, whom they had not seen before, ran unto them (157)."

Capture of Nicholas Owen

There could be no doubt about the identity of these pale, unshaven, tottering spectres, and they were instantly seized. This success made the searchers begin "afresh to search more violently than ever . . . for five or six days (158)." As it turned out their persistence paid dividends, for on 30th January two

New Palace Yard in London. Strict laws were passed after the discovery of the Gunpowder Plot, and Catholics were not allowed to live in or near London

Jesuit priests emerged from yet another hidden chamber.

Father Garnet surrenders

It was not starvation that defeated these two, but the discomforts of their hole: "The place was so close those customs of nature which must of necessity be done and in so long time of continuance was exceedingly offensive to the men themselves and did much annoy them that they had not been able to hold out one whole day longer, but either they must have squealed or perished in that place. The whole service endured the space of eleven nights and twelve days (159)."

As Red Humphrey had thought, one of these men was Father Oldcorne. The other was the richest prize that Robert Cecil could have hoped for, Father Henry Garnet, the Superior of the English Jesuits. He, like the Gunpowder Plot conspirators before him, became the centre-piece of a political show trial, and the victim of Sir Edward Coke, the Attorney General. Like them he was executed, on 3rd May, 1606.

Laws against the Catholics

Within a few weeks of Garnet's death Parliament had passed two laws against the Catholics. One was called "An Act for the better discovering and repressing of Catholic Recusants," and the other was "An Act to prevent and avoid dangers which may grow by Popish Recusants." Their many clauses were so severe that it seems strange that Catholicism should have survived. They struck at every level of Catholic life and at all social classes.

Catholics were not allowed to appear at Court, or live in or near London. They could not travel from their homes without a magistrate's permission. They were forbidden to be doctors or lawyers, and other professions were also closed to them. Their homes could be searched almost at will, and they could neither be guests nor servants of Protestants. Anyone who failed to take communion from a Protestant minister at least once a year was fined. Wealthy Catholics, who had been ready to pay fines to avoid attending Protestant churches, now found that two-thirds of their property might be confiscated for this offence.

The reason why Catholicism survived despite these laws was that they were not regularly enforced. As soon as the panic caused by the Plot died down King James was inclined to relax the thorough administration of this penal code. He was too

Overleaf An allegorical picture showing the expulsion of the Jesuits

Arnaudus Advo
Parisie
ad S.RŪS!

P. Collowrat.
P. Hayrol.
P. Faninus.
Pater Forro.
Curriæ
P. Caldi.
P. Rumer.

Sir Edward Coke, the Attorney General

lenient for the liking of the House of Commons, and in 1610 they were urging him "to lay your royal command upon all your ministers of justice, both ecclesiastical and civil, to see the laws made against Jesuits, seminary priests, and recusants . . . be duly executed without dread or delay."

Dramatis Personae

BATES, Thomas (d. 1606). Catesby's servant, and the one conspirator who was not ranked as a gentleman. After the explosion at Holbeach House he fled, was captured, and executed for treason. His evidence was used to falsely implicate the Jesuits in the Plot.

CATESBY, Robert (1573–1605). Warwickshire gentleman who took part in the Essex Rebellion, and subsequently originated the Gunpowder Plot. Killed in the fight at Holbeach House.

CECIL, Robert, Earl of Salisbury (1563?–1612). Secretary of State to Elizabeth I and James I. Violently anti-Catholic, he supervised the destruction of the Plot and those concerned in it.

COKE, Sir Edward (1552–1634). Brilliant lawyer who, as Attorney General, prosecuted the conspirators and Father Garnet.

DIGBY, Sir Everard (1581–1606). Wealthy and talented. Catesby chose him to lead the Midland Rebellion that would follow the blowing-up of Parliament. He fled from Holbeach House, was captured, and executed.

FAWKES, Guy (1570–1606). Yorkshireman, and a soldier in Flanders from 1593–1604. Captured with the gunpowder he was to use to blow up Parliament, tortured, and executed.

GARNET, Father Henry (1554–1606). Derbyshire man, and head

of the English Jesuits for nineteen years. Opposed to the Plot, although friendly with the conspirators. Betrayed, captured at Hindlip House, falsely implicated in the Plot, and executed.

JAMES I (1566–1625). Tolerant by nature, his persecution of the Catholics was largely due to pressure from Parliament. But as he believed in the Divine Right of Kings, and as his father had been assassinated by gunpowder, the Plot obviously affected him deeply.

PARKER, William, Lord Monteagle (1575–1622). A veteran of the Essex Rebellion, brother-in-law to Francis Tresham, he was a convert from Catholicism. Received the letter by which, according to the government, the Plot was revealed.

PERCY, Thomas (1560–1605). Cousin to the Earl of Northumberland, and the only aristocrat among the conspirators. One of Catesby's first helpers. Killed at Holbeach House.

ROOKWOOD, Ambrose (1579–1606). Suffolk gentleman and famous horseman, brought into the Plot partly because of his wealth. Fled from Holbeach House, captured, and executed.

TRESHAM, Francis (1567?–1605). A veteran of the Essex Rebellion, of doubtful character, brought into the Plot partly because of his wealth. Probably betrayed the Plot. Imprisoned, and died mysteriously in the Tower of London, probably by poison.

WINTER, Thomas (1572–1606). Worcestershire gentleman, soldier in Flanders and traveller, one of the first conspirators. Capture at Holbeach House and executed.

Table of Dates

1603	
March	James VI of Scotland becomes James I of England
1604	
February	Robert Catesby first discusses a Plot with Thomas Winter
April	Thomas Winter's diplomatic mission to the Constable of Castile in Flanders
May (?)	Catesby, Winter, Percy, Fawkes and John Wright swear an oath of secrecy
24th May	Percy obtains the lease of John Whynniard's house
August	Constable of Castile comes to England and confirms Anglo-Spanish peace treaty
September	Government enforces anti-Catholic laws
11th December	Conspirators begin their tunnelling operations
1605	
25th March	Conspirators obtain the lease of the room immediately below the Lords' Chamber
March	Robert Winter, John Grant and Ambrose Rookwood admitted to the Plot
June	Catesby and Father Garnet discuss the morality of killing
July	Father Tesimond learns about the Plot from Catesby, and confesses his knowledge to Garnet
August	Sir Everard Digby admitted to the Plot
9th October	Francis Tresham admitted to the Plot

24th October	Robert Cecil's letter to Sir Thomas Lake, indicating that he knows about the Plot
26th October	"The little comedy at Hoxton" – the discovery of the Gunpowder Plot
28th October	Winter warns Catesby that the Plot is discovered, and that they should leave England
30th October	Guy Fawkes tells Catesby that the gunpowder is still undetected
4th November	Digby moves to Coughton Court, his base for the Midland Rising
	Guy Fawkes arrested
5th November	Digby holds his hunting match on Dunsmore Heath
	Plotters fly from London and reach Catesby's house at Ashby St. Legers
8th November	Accidental explosion of gunpowder at Holbeach House
	Arrival of Sheriff's posse and attack on Plotters
9th November	King James announces the Plot to Parliament
10th November	Day of Thanksgiving in London churches
12th November	Francis Tresham arrested
23rd December	Tresham dies mysteriously while under arrest

1606

9th January	Capture of Robert Winter, the last Plotter at large
19th January	Sheriff's posse searches Hindlip House for Jesuits
26th January	Capture of two lay Jesuits at Hindlip
27th January	Trial of surviving Plotters
30th January	Capture of Fathers Garnet and Oldcorne at Hindlip
30th/31st January	Execution of Plotters
28th March	Trial of Father Garnet
3rd May	Execution of Father Garnet

Further Reading

Gunpowder Treason and Plot is a simplification of a very complex incident. Other modern books on the subject usually set out to plead a particular case. The most straightforward account is Hugh Ross Williamson's *The Gunpowder Plot* (1951) which is thorough and well documented, but it is not easy reading. Other works, listed alphabetically, include: Father Philip Caraman, *Henry Garnet* (1555–1606) *and the Gunpowder Plot* (1964); Paul Durst, *Intended Treason* (1970); Father Francis Edwards, *Guy Fawkes – The Real Story of the Gunpowder Plot?* (1969); Henry Garnett, *Portrait of Guy Fawkes* (1962); E. N. Simons, *The Devil of the Vault* (1963).

Picture Credits

The author and publishers wish to thank the following for permission to reproduce the copyright illustrations that appear on the pages mentioned. Mansell collection, jacket, 20–21, 22–23, 29, 50, 51, 58–59, 80–81, 98–99, 104–105; Radio Times Hulton Picture Library, 10, 15, 16–17, 19, 28, 33, 38, 40, 43, 44, 46–47, 57, 65, 66, 68, 72, 75, 76, 84, 87, 90–91, 92, 94–95, 100, 107, 112–113, 114; Trustees of the British Museum, 110. Other illustrations are the property of the Wayland Picture Library.

List of Sources

(1) J. Gerard, *What was the Gunpowder Plot?* (1897), p. 234
(2) G. Goodman, *The Court of King James the First* (1839), I, p. 101
(3) Public Records Office, Roman Transcripts (Bliss), No. 86, cited by H. R. Williamson, *The Gunpowder Plot* (1951), p. 16
(4) Williamson, p. 20
(5) A. G. Dickens and D. Carr, *The Reformation in England to the Accession of Elizabeth I* (1969), p. 65
(6) G. A Williamson, *Foxe's Book of Martyrs* (1965) p. xxxi
(7) H. Bettenson, *Documents of the Christian World* (1943), pp. 338–39
(8) *Ibid*
(9) B. Basset, *The English Jesuits* (1967), p. 16
(10) *Letters and Memorials of Fr. Robert Persons S. J.*, cited by H. R. Williamson, p. 27
(11) Basset, p. 2
(12) J. Morris, *Father Gerard's Narrative of the Gunpowder Plot* (1871), pp. 36–39
(13) Sir A. Weldon, *Court and Character of King James* (1811), II, pp. 1–2
(14) Morris, p. 20
(15) W. McElwee, *The Wisest Fool in Christendom* (1960), p. 131
(16) *Ibid*
(17) *Correspondence of King James VI of Scotland with Sir Robert Cecil and others in England,* Camden Society (1861), p. 56
(18) *Ibid*
(19) Calendar of State Papers, Venetian, 1603–1607, p. 10
(20) Miscellanea, II, Catholic Record Society, p. 213
(21) D. H. Willson, *King James VI and I* (1956), p. 222
(22) Historical Manuscripts Commission, Hatfield MSS, XV, p. 264
(23) Calendar of State Papers, Domestic, James I, LXIX, p. 56
(24) CSPV, 1603–1607, p. 230
(25) Morris, pp. 54–57
(26) *Ibid*, pp. 57–58
(27) *Ibid*, p. 59
(28) *Ibid*, pp. 58–59
(29) W. Cobbett, *State Trials* (1809), II, p. 204
(30) *Ibid*
(31) *Ibid*
(32) *Ibid*
(33) *Ibid*
(34) *Ibid*, p. 205
(35) D. Jardine, *A Narrative of the Gunpowder Plot* (1857), p. 38
(36) Cobbett, p. 206
(37) *Ibid*
(38) *Ibid*, p. 206
(39) T. Fuller, *The Church History of Britain* (1845), X, p. 35
(40) Cobbett, p. 207
(41) *Ibid*, p. 206
(42) *Ibid*, p. 202
(43) *Ibid*
(44) *Ibid*, p. 207
(45) *Ibid*
(46) *Ibid*, p. 203
(47) *Ibid*, p. 207

(48) *Ibid*
(49) *Ibid*
(50) *Ibid*
(51) *Ibid*, p. 208
(52) *Ibid*, p. 187
(53) *Morris*, pp. 88–89
(54) *Ibid*, p. 89
(55) *Cobbett*, p. 186
(56) *Morris*, p. 86
(57) *Ibid*
(58) *Ibid*, pp. 90–91
(59) Cobbett, p. 175
(60) CSPD, *Gunpowder Plot Book*, 136
(61) *Ibid*
(62) Hatfield MSS, XVIII, p. 107
(63) *Ibid*
(64) Morris, p. 71
(65) *Ibid*, p. 72
(66) T. Longueville, *The Life of a Conspirator* (1895), p. 137
(67) Morris, p. 77
(68) Sir R. Winwood, *Memorials of Affairs of State* (1725), II, p. 68
(69) Morris, p. 79
(70) Hatfield MSS, XVII, p. 258
(71) *Ibid*, p. 320
(72) CSPD GPB, p. 237
(73) CSPD, James I, LXIX, p. 306
(74) Cobbett, p. 195
(75) *Ibid*, p. 197
(76) *Ibid*, p. 195
(77) *Ibid*, p. 196
(78) *Ibid*, p. 198
(79) H. R. Williamson, p. 156
(80) Cobbett, p. 199
(81) *Ibid*
(82) *Ibid*
(83) *Ibid*
(84) *Ibid*, p. 209
(85) *Ibid*
(86) Morris, p. 102
(87) *Ibid*
(88) *Ibid*, p. 100–101
(89) CSPD GPB, p. 126
(90) *Ibid*, p. 135
(91) *Ibid*, p. 126
(92) T. Barlow, *The Gunpowder Treason* (1850), p. 251
(93) Cobbett, p. 209
(94) *Ibid*, pp. 200–201
(95) *Ibid*, p. 201
(96) *Ibid*
(97) *Ibid*, p. 209
(98) *Ibid*
(99) CSPD GPB, 176
(100) H. R. Williamson, p. 174
(101) CSPD GPB, 121
(102) *Ibid*, 136
(103) H. R. Williamson, p. 176
(104) *Ibid*
(105) CSPD GPB, 108 and 119
(106) H. R. Williamson, p. 178
(107) Cobbett, p. 182
(108) *Ibid*, p. 210
(109) Morris, p. 108
(110) *Ibid*
(111) Cobbett, p. 210
(112) CSPD GPB, 55
(113) H. R. Williamson, p. 181
(114) Morris, p. 109
(115) Cobbett, p. 210
(116) Hatfield MSS, XVII, p. 518
(117) *Ibid*
(118) H. R. Williamson, p. 186
(119) *Ibid*, p. 187
(120) *Ibid*, p. 185
(121) Hatfield MSS, XVII, p. 518
(122) CSPD, James I, XVI, p. 241
(123) Winwood, II, p. 172
(124) Hatfield MSS, XVII, p. 479
(125) *Ibid*
(126) *Ibid*
(127) CSPD, James I, XVI, p. 241
(128) *Ibid*, p. 246
(129) *Ibid*, p. 247
(130) Hatfield MSS, XVII, p. 541
(131) Goodman, I, p. 107
(132) H. R. Williamson, p. 198
(133) *Ibid*
(134) CSPD GPB, 145
(135) Morris, p. 136
(136) *Ibid*
(137) Cobbett, p. 166
(138) *Ibid*
(139) *Ibid*, p. 176
(140) *Ibid*, p. 184
(141) Longueville, p. 291
(142) Hatfield MSS, XVIII, p. 36
(143) Morris, p. 219
(144) Cobbett, p. 217
(145) *Ibid*, p. 218
(146) Hatfield MSS, XVII, p. 531
(147) *Ibid*, p. 511
(148) *Ibid*, p. 485
(149) *Ibid*, p. 520–601
(150) *Ibid*, p. 520
(151) *Ibid*, p. 591
(152) *Ibid*, p. 490
(153) Hatfield MSS, XVIII, p. 269
(154) *Ibid*, XVII, p. 540
(155) *Ibid*, XVIII, p. 35
(156) Morris, pp. 151–2
(157) *Ibid*, p. 153
(158) *Ibid*, 157
(159) H. R. Williamson, p. 229

Index